PENGUIN BOOKS

RESILIENCE

Boris Cyrulnik is an internationally renowned psychologist and leading proponent of the theory of resilience: that we are much more capable of overcoming traumatic events in our lives than we imagine. Working with genocide victims in Rwanda and child soldiers in Colombia, he travels around the world helping individuals and countries come to terms with their pasts to create positive new outlooks. He is the author of numerous books on resilience (including *Talking of Love*, also published by Penguin) and its possibilities in childhood and throughout life. An international best-seller, his work has been credited with helping France heal the wounds left by the Second World War. Cyrulnik was born in 1937; in 1942 his parents were deported to a concentration camp and never returned. Maltreated by his foster parents, he was eventually chosen as a runner in the liberation, perilously crossing enemy lines to deliver messages to French fighters. He was seven. This personal trauma helped him develop his belief that trauma is not destiny.

Resilience

How Your Inner Strength
Can Set You Free From The Past

Boris Cyrulnik

TRANSLATED BY

DAVID MACEY

PENGUIN BOOKS

PENGUIN BOOKS

Published by the Penguin Group
Penguin Books Ltd, 80 Strand, London WC2R ORL, England
Penguin Group (USA) Inc., 375 Hudson Street, New York, New York 10014, USA
Penguin Group (Canada), 90 Eglinton Avenue East, Suite 700, Toronto, Ontario, Canada M4P 2Y3
(a division of Pearson Penguin Canada Inc.)
Penguin Ireland, 25 St Stephen's Green, Dublin 2, Ireland (a division of Penguin Books Ltd)
Penguin Group (Australia), 250 Camberwell Road, Camberwell, Victoria 3124, Australia
(a division of Pearson Australia Group Pty Ltd)
Penguin Books India Pvt Ltd, 11 Community Centre, Panchsheel Park, New Delhi – 110 017, India
Penguin Group (NZ), 67 Apollo Drive, Rosedale, North Shore 0632, New Zealand
(a division of Pearson New Zealand Ltd)
Penguin Books (South Africa) (Pty) Ltd, 24 Sturdee Avenue, Rosebank,
Johannesburg 2196, South Africa

Penguin Books Ltd, Registered Offices: 80 Strand, London WC2R ORL, England

www.penguin.com

This translation first published by Penguin Books 2009

3

Copyright © Boris Cyrulnik, 2009
Translator's copyright © David Macey, 2009
All rights reserved

The moral right of the author and translator has been asserted

This book is supported by the French Ministry of Foreign Affairs, as part of the Burgess
programme run by the Cultural Department of the French Embassy in London.

Liberté · Égalité · Fraternité
RÉPUBLIQUE FRANÇAISE

Typeset in Fournier MT 14/16.15pt by Palimpsest Book Production Limited,
Grangemouth, Stirlingshire
Printed in England by Clays Ltd, St Ives plc

978-0-141-03615-1

www.greenpenguin.co.uk

Mixed Sources
Product group from well-managed
forests and other controlled sources
www.fsc.org Cert no. SA-COC-1592
© 1996 Forest Stewardship Council
FSC

Penguin Books is committed to a sustainable future
for our business, our readers and our planet.
The book in your hands is made from paper
certified by the Forest Stewardship Council.

Contents

I

Introduction:
Resilience as a natural process

Misfortunes are never wonderful. But when an ordeal does come, do we have to succumb to it? And if we fight it, what weapons do we have?

We are astonished when we meet children who triumph over their misfortunes

There is nothing new about this amazement. We have always been astonished by children who succeed in surviving terrible ordeals and making something of themselves even against all the odds. Yet the classic way in which the statement is made shows that it has been interpreted even before it has been studied. We are 'astonished' because they have 'triumphed' over an immense 'misfortune'. The implication 'wonderful' is already associated with 'misfortune'. Yet if 'triumph' can be observed, the misfortune must have been overcome, and the wounded child must have had time to write a few chapters of his history by looking back at his past in order to explain to himself how he survived.

It is not until much later, not until we have reached the age of reason, that we can relate the meaning of 'triumph' to a chaotic childhood. And yet, at the very moment the misfortune occurs, the demoralized child's feelings are confused: he has been hurt, but he is still hopeful. As soon as he is hurt, the child begins to dream of a better future: 'I'll get over it in time . . . I'll get my own back one day . . . I'll show them.' And because the pleasure of the dream becomes linked with the painful reality, he is able to withstand it. It is even possible that the torment heightens the need to imagine a future: 'Muddy paths often make the spiritual dawn more desirable and the need for an ideal more persistent.'[1]

There is no such thing as pure unhappiness, or pure happiness. But as soon as we put sadness into a story, we give a meaning to our sufferings and understand, long after the event, how we succeeded in turning our unhappiness into something wonderful. Anyone who has been hurt has to undergo a metamorphosis. 'I learned to turn unhappiness into a test. One makes you bow your head, but the other makes you hold your head up high,' explains Catherine Enjolet, who was born in 1954 and brought up in care.[2] In 1990, she founded the charity Parrains par mille (Godparents by the Thousand), which encourages the volunteer monitoring of deprived children in the community.

Two words govern the way we observe and understand the mystery of those who have survived and who, as adults, can look back at the scars left by their past. The words that teach us how to look are 'resilience' and, less obviously, 'oxymoron'.

When the word 'resilience' was first used in physics it referred to a body's ability to absorb an impact. But for our purposes this attaches too much importance to the body's substance. When it began to be used in the social sciences, it came to mean 'The ability to succeed, to live and to develop in a positive and socially acceptable way, despite the stress or adversity that would normally involve the real possibility of a negative outcome'.[3]

How do we become human despite the blows of fate? We have been asking that question ever since we began to try to discover the lost continent of childhood. The nice little Rémi raises the problem in very clear terms in Henri Malot's novel *Sans Famille* (1878): 'I am a foundling. But I believed that, like all the other children, I did have a mother.'[4] Two volumes later, having lived on the streets and been exploited at work, beaten, robbed and ill, Rémi wins his right to lead a socially acceptable life in London and ends his story with a Neapolitan song that evokes 'soft words' and the 'right to love'. The rules of the genre are precisely the same as in Charles Dickens, who drew on the wretched childhood in which he was exploited to develop his themes of suffering and victory over suffering. 'I saw no reason ... why the dregs of life ... should not serve the purpose of a mortal, as well as its froth and cream ... It involved the best and worst shades of our nature; much of its ugliest hues and something of its most beautiful.'⁵ 'When we read Tolstoy's *Youth*, we always think of that line from Aragon: "Is this how men live?"'⁶ Maxim Gorky's account of his childhood traces the same archetypal journey from the desolation of Act I (*Childhood*, 1913–14), to the reparation of Act II (*In the World*, 1915–16) and the triumph of Act III (*My Universities*, 1923). All these popular novels illustrate the same idea: our sufferings are not in vain, and victory is always possible.

This theme is taken up as though it were a fundamental need, or the only hope of those who are without hope:

> If you can make one heap of all your winnings
> And risk it on one turn of pitch-and-toss,
> And hope and start again at your beginnings
> And never breathe a word about your loss ...
> You'll be a Man, my son!⁷

At the end of the short story by Jules Renard the abused child nicknamed 'Carrots' or 'Carrot Top' (*Poil de carotte*) learns to hope again;⁸ Hervé Bazin finds peace when his father finally makes Foloche shut up;⁹ Tarzan, who was a child at risk in a hostile jungle, ends up becoming the beloved leader of fearsome animals; Zorro and Superman, who are insignificant figures in real life, triumph over the baddies and restore justice. Some of François Truffaut's films tell the story of his disrupted childhood, while the singer Jean-Luc Lahaye describes how he was brought up in care in his *Cent Familles*.[10] In *City of Joy* Dominique Lapierre describes the astonishing cheerfulness of Calcutta's wretched street kids,[11] and anyone who has had dealings with such children will confirm the accuracy of his description.[12]

When the wounded child becomes the subject of a novel and the object of a science

These social fairy tales in fact bear witness to the birth of the popular novel in an industrial civilization. They give hope to those who have been mistreated, and they all carry the same message: 'Do not pity us. Our laughter is a weapon. We are stronger than despair.'

In the twentieth century the specialists gathered around the cradle, and the child became a scientific object. The paediatrician's biological child has nothing to do with the psychologist's symbolic child. Psychologists know nothing about children in institutional care and are astounded by the great relativity of the historian's child.

The Second World War represented a real cultural revolution in child observation. Anna Freud noticed that some children who were very damaged when she took them into Hampstead Nursery grew up to be adults who appeared to flourish.[13] Françoise Dolto confirms her observations: 'And yet there are human beings who have, because of their fate or some incident that occurred during their childhood, been deprived of the presence of either their mother or of both parents. They can grow up to be as healthy and sturdy . . . as children who had an integrated family structure, but will display different characteristics.'[14]

From the 1960s onwards those studying the problem of resilience began to look at protective factors.[15] Although their lives are chaotic, resilient children begin to use internal defence mechanisms at a very early age. These may include splitting – that is, splitting the ego into a socially acceptable part and a more hidden side that expresses itself in roundabout and surprising ways. A split personality will say 'You're right, but all the same . . .'[16] Denial allows us to ignore a dangerous reality, or to make light of a painful wound: 'No, no, it's not paraplegia at all.' Daydreams are so beautiful when the real world is desolate: 'I used to wait impatiently for night to come so that I could be alone with my dreams again.' We can imagine wonderful refuges by breaking off relationships that are too difficult. Intellectualization allows us to avoid confrontations in which we might become personally involved. 'Calm down, I'm not talking about you. I'm talking about aggressors who . . .' Abstraction forces us to discover the general laws that allow us to defeat or avoid our enemies, whereas the absence of danger induces intellectual numbness.

Human beings can, finally, transform a situation at a stroke, and turn an oppressive tragedy into mild euphoria: 'I have learned from experience that humour is not all that far removed from death, lies, humility, loneliness, unbearable and sustained tenderness, a distrust of appearances, keeping secrets, keeping one's distance, and screams of protest against injustice.'[17] When François Billetdoux, whose very name suggests humour, unbearable tenderness and deadly secrets, wrote those lines, he could not have known that they might serve as a description of Roberto Benigni's Holocaust comedy *La Vita è bella* (1998). Whilst the film does not turn Auschwitz into a joke, it certainly does illustrate the protective function of humour . . . and what it costs the individuals concerned: Act I: The fairground atmosphere is a mixture of humour and cheerfulness; the aggressor is comic, without realizing it. Act II: Fortunately, the victims have a sense of humour. That allows them to put up with an unbearable situation. Act III: The survivors win. 'I nearly died laughing.'[18] The last line of the film tells us something about the ambivalence of defence mechanisms: they protect us, but there is a price to be paid.

We nearly die laughing when Georges Perec cites learned articles such as 'Deterioration of the ego in pets (*Arch. Psychiat. Animal*, 66, 1958: 35–38)', 'Presence of cannabinol in freeze-dried broccoli (*Bull. Trim. Lab. Pol. Judic.* 159, 1979: 975–1007)' and 'A scientific and literary friendship: Léon Burp and Marcel Gotlib, followed by a new consideration of the life and work of Romauld Saint-Sahaint (preface to the second, privately printed, volume of the *Complete Works of Gotlib*, 1980)'.[19] His humour in fact makes mockery of the violence of the administration's fundamentalists, who kill because that is what the rules tell them to do. That's how it is. No need for scruples, as in *W, or The Memory of Childhood*, which recounts how the organizers of the solemn Olympiads have athletes who do not win put to death, because that is the rule.[20] 'You very quickly get used to living a peaceful life in a place where hundreds of thousands of people are being gassed. It had no effect on me,' recalled Hans Münch, who was assistant to Dr Mengele, the Auschwitz experimenter and 'the most agreeable of companions'.[21]

Dictators force the people to be happy, but they do not like the people's sense of humour because it is a sign of the struggle against suffering: 'The October Group was awarded a prize for its production of Jacques Prévert's first play *La Bataille de Fontenoy* ... much to the annoyance of Stalin, who held that a happy people, such as the Soviet people, did not need a sense of humour.'[22] When the pain is too great, we cannot perceive anything else. We are just in pain. But as soon as we can distance ourselves from it and turn it into a play, the unhappiness becomes bearable, though it would be more accurate to say that it is transformed into laughter or a work of art. That is why Anne Frank's diary enjoyed such popularity after the war, at a time when no one wanted to listen to direct eye-witness accounts.[23] They were intolerable because they made us neither laugh nor cry. They were pure horror, and did not bear thinking about. When it cannot sublimate things, culture denies their existence: 'But if I can change the way you see me, then I can change the way I feel about myself.' This is a defence mechanism on a knife edge because, if I succeed in making you laugh at my misfortunes, I can prove to myself that I am once more in control of my past and that I am not such a victim after all. Because it refuses 'to be distressed by the provocations of reality',[24] the ego can control both the way its misfortunes are depicted and the wounded soul's narrative identity: 'I am no longer the man who was tortured . . . I am becoming a man who can transform the memory of his sufferings into an acceptable work of art.'

The fact that resilience has not been studied even though most if not all practitioners are familiar with the phenomenon says a lot about our culture, which still views survivors with suspicion. 'It's because they colluded with the enemy that they didn't die like all the rest. Only the victims are innocent.' This cut-and-dried argument uses the language of Manichaeism. It takes no account of the ambivalence of our inner worlds, where we sometimes hate those we really love and try to find a trace of humanity in our worst enemies.

Towards the end of his life John Bowlby, one of the founders of the attachment theory that now enjoys such popularity, expressed the hope that more work would begin to be done on resilience. Psychology, he used to say, is based upon the implicit assumption that the harder one's life is, the more likely one is to suffer from depression.[25] This is far from certain. Certainly, the harder our lives are, the more difficulty we will find in living them; but suffering and sadness are not in themselves signs of depression.

What is more, we do not remain the same, for we are always growing older. The same event will have a different effect depending on when it occurs. Someone losing their mother at the age of six months falls into a void, into a sensorial nothingness, until such time as a substitute takes the mother's place. There is a danger that the child will die. Someone losing their mother at the age of six becomes someone who no longer has a mother, and is transformed into a 'child-minus'. There is a danger that some psycho-emotional damage will be done, that the child's sense of identity will be distorted. Someone losing their mother at the age of sixty realizes that such a loss is almost inevitable. The danger is metaphysical.

Traumas always strike differently because they occur at different times and affect different psychic constructs.

The fact that all traumas are different suggests that history is not destiny

Our history does not determine our destiny. What is written does not remain written for long. What is true today will no longer be true tomorrow because human determinisms work in the short term. Our sufferings force us to undergo a metamorphosis and we always hope that we will be able to change the way we live our lives. That is why early deprivation creates a momentary vulnerability, and why our emotional or social encounters can either cure it or make it worse.

In that sense, resilience is a natural process: what we are at any given moment obliges us to use our ecological, emotional and verbal environments to 'knit' ourselves. We might feel that, if a single stitch is dropped, everything will unravel, but in fact, if just one stitch holds, we can start all over again.

At the traumatic moment, of course, we perceive only the wound. It is not until much later that we can speak of resilience; not until the restored adult can at last come to terms with the chaos of her childhood. We succumb to the retrospective illusion, believe everything we see and talk about her social restoration, but we do not know what is going on in the inner world of the adult who has 'succeeded' despite everything.

We must, however, approach the problem from both sides. Seen from the outside, resilience is so common that it proves that we can survive. Seen from the inside, the fact that we are structured like an oxymoron reveals that the internal world of the wounded individual is divided into two. Heaven and Hell cohabit, and happiness is balanced on a knife edge.

In an attempt to elucidate the mystery of how resilience is knitted, British and American psychologists, who have handed down the optimistic credo of 'I have, I think, I am' from one generation to the next,[26] carried out fieldwork by living with children whose souls had been wounded and observing their development. Two hundred children who were at serious parental and social risk were followed up on a regular basis on the island of Kawai, which is near Hawaii. A few decades later 130 of them were found to have gone on to lead lives that were catastrophic in medical, psycho-emotional and social terms. This confirms the importance of environmental factors. But no one was interested in what became of the seventy children who grew up to be cheerful, fully rounded and good social actors despite the ordeal of their earliest years.

Eleven children identified by the American welfare services were followed up on a regular basis for the next fifty years. Regular appointments meant that their physical, psycho-emotional, intellectual and social state could be recorded.[27] When the study began, they were all damaged. By the time they had reached adolescence, there were still major risk factors, but most of them were observed to have organized resilience factors: some were becoming independent, whilst others displayed a gift for relationships, creativity and humour. Several of these adolescents were, despite their difficult childhood, greatly concerned with ethics, which goes to prove that they were not destined to repeat their past. By the age of forty-five, five of the eleven children had become well-rounded adults. The three who had failed to do so were not the ones who had suffered the most violence, but those who had been most isolated and who had had the least support.

Over the last ten to twenty years a growing body of work has confirmed the impressions of practitioners, all of whom are familiar with case histories demonstrating that survival is possible and that the future is not so bleak, provided that a few development guidelines are given.[28]

Some sixty children placed in foster families were followed on a regular basis until they were twenty-five.[29] Over half (56 per cent) were thriving: they were in good health, enjoyed their jobs, and were living in stable relationships. Their children were blossoming. Of the rest, 12 per cent were struggling to a greater or lesser extent and 32 per cent had medical, psycho-emotional or social problems. The lives of this small group are only slightly more difficult than those of the population at large; 23 per cent of all young people experience physical, psychological or social problems. Things are obviously much more difficult for those whose childhood has been shattered, but this is far from being the transgenerational tragedy of contemporary social discourse.[30]

Until now, research has been concentrated on how the damage was done: there is no denying that the damage was done, but we now have to look at how it can be repaired

For our purposes, the interesting thing is that almost all the children who did survive very quickly elaborated 'theories of life' that combined dreams and intellectualization. Almost all resilient children have to answer two questions. Asking 'Why do I have to suffer so much?' encourages them to intellectualize. 'How am I going to manage to be happy despite it all?' is an invitation to dream. If this inner determinant of resilience can find a helping hand, the prognosis for these children is not unfavourable.

The adults who were in the most pain were the children of parents who were mentally ill or abusive, and children who did not succeed in finding emotional substitutes, perhaps because they felt too great a responsibility towards the adults who had damaged them. That does not mean they might not have survived, but it does confirm that no link was established between their inner and outer worlds.

There is nothing inevitable about the repetition of the past. But the repetition does become problematic when, because it believes that these children's destiny is inevitable, society abandons them to their wretched fate. The outcome is a self-fulfilling prophecy. Not to mention the fact that the figures that provide the prophecy with its ammunition are themselves the product of three serious misunderstandings.

The problem is that the professionals only come into contact with those who repeat the abuse. They overlook the rest because resilient children cope with their wounds and stay out of the social welfare system.

The second mistake is that the converse is not true. Whilst it is quite true that many abusive parents were abused as children, it is not true that children who have been abused will become abusive parents.[31]

The fact that its findings are inconsistent does not mean that the research is incoherent. On the contrary, it proves that the effects of childhood wounds depend largely on the different ways in which the environment is organized. When, after the Second World War, children who had been abandoned became parents, they often abandoned their children in their turn and put them in foster care, just as they had been. Because their sociocultural situation was catastrophic, their own histories suggested to them that they should abandon their children. But since the 1980s there have been almost no repeat placements because social and emotional institutions now provide such people with more support.

The third mistake is to divide the inner and outer worlds to such an extent as to make us believe that individuals can escape their context. Now, the reason why an event is imprinted on the subjective memory of an individual is that it has been highlighted by the emotional reactions of those around him or her, or because his or her culture sees it as something important. The same behavioural scenario can take on very different meanings, depending on the social context. Drug dealing is regarded as a crime by people who have been socialized, but it can also be a life-saver; for people who have been socially humiliated it can result in reparation or even resilience. Children who live in neighbourhoods that are wallowing in social and cultural poverty are constantly being humiliated. They perform badly at school, either because their families often do not see the importance of education, or because they have to work in the evenings to make money. When violence rules the streets, they are often beaten up or threatened because they are weak. Society, in its turn, excludes them, leaves them unemployed and stresses their constant failures. And then one day a dealer teaches them that they can earn enough money to win back their dignity in just one night. The very next morning they give their family money and can lord it over the kids who used to bully them.[32] In social and cultural terms they have no future, but delinquency allows them to become resilient. They make reparation to themselves by making reparation to their families and rediscover their dignity by becoming delinquent. For the street children of Bogotá or São Paulo, this is a classic survival strategy. A little boy who refuses to become delinquent stands a very good chance of being killed. The ones who do have a talent for delinquency, which is valuable in such a context, do so well that they can buy huge estates, finance private armies and send their children to elite schools where they receive an excellent education. These resilient kids certainly do not repeat the social abuse they have suffered, as their children never take drugs and because, in a context such as this, having a criminal father is a stroke of social luck.

The ability to knit together a feeling of selfhood appears to be a major factor in the aptitude for resilience. Now, the feeling of selfhood is an emotion that is experienced physically, and its origins lie in social representations: insulting a child by calling him a 'bastard' does not give rise to the same feeling as telling him he is the son of a prince. Which comes down to saying that the emotion a child feels and expresses through his behaviour is determined by social discourse.

In 1994 there were 200,000 Holocaust survivors aged about sixty-five in Israel.[33] Twenty-eight per cent survived the camps, 58 per cent were hidden and almost 10 per cent fought in the resistance movement, even though they were very young. It so happens that, after the war, all these children, with the exception of those who fought in the armed resistance, were depressed for several years.

The data is difficult to interpret. Did these children join the resistance movement because they were already more resilient? Did the feeling of belonging that bound the resistance fighters together protect them from depression? Or did their narrative identity, or the stories they rehearsed in their heads after the war – 'I am the boy who, at the age of eight, stood up to the German army' – give them a feeling of selfhood that had more in common with a hero than a victim? If it is true that resilience is something we knit, all these factors are associated. But what is true at one point in someone's life is not true at another point because it no longer has the same effects. It so happens that post-war depression was most common in the sub-group of children who were deported when they were about five, and that is not surprising. But the same sub-group was also the most successful in terms of their family and professional lives. There was no incidence of depression in the sub-group of children who fought with the armed resistance. But when they became adults, the little heroes were content with mediocre social positions. That was enough to make them happy because they found it easy to lead a quiet life. In contrast, the children who were deported had to make a success of their family lives and social adventures if they wanted to recover from the terrible wounds that had been inflicted on them in the camps. Their post-war depression forced them to overinvest in the emotional life of their families and in social success. Their depression forced them to look for happiness. This oxymoron really is the price we have to pay for resilience.

A victorious defence costs only a few oxymorons

An oxymoron is a rhetorical figure that associates two antinomic or contradictory terms. Milton's 'darkness visible' and Corneille's *obscure clarté* are two famous examples.[34] When the adjective 'wonderful' is applied to an object we do not expect – 'misfortune' – the figure makes it possible to express an antithesis. This is not the same as ambivalence, in which the subject expresses the conflicting emotions of love and hate for the same person: 'A battle between love and hate was raging in the lover's breast, and the object of both these feelings was one and the same person.'[35] That feeling is especially clear in jealousy, as when Othello wants to kill the woman he loves above all others in order to possess her completely, or as when a child bites its mother in loving exasperation. Ambivalence is characteristic of an instinctive movement towards a love-object we desire and which attaches us to it, or even imprisons us. An oxymoron, in contrast, reveals the conflicting emotions of someone who, having suffered a major blow, adapts to it by splitting. The part of the personality that has been hurt suffers and bears a scar, but another part, which is better protected, still unhurt but more hidden, uses the energy of despair to bring together anything that can still produce some happiness and give some meaning to life. When we adapt to a disaster, therefore, we associate gangrene with beauty and dung with flowers. When Gérard de Nerval speaks of 'the black sun of melancholy' he is not contrasting two sensations but associating them, just like the melancholy patients who say they are fascinated by the horrible wonder of death: it is 'horrible' because they are afraid of their own desire for death, and it is 'wonderful' because they are hoping for an end to their suffering. Each term highlights the other, and the contrast between them emphasizes both. The oxymoron becomes characteristic of a personality that has been wounded but which still resists, that suffers but is happy enough to go on hoping despite everything. It is the cornerstone in the history of a wound. As André Ughetto explains, the same thing happens in Gothic architecture: 'the arches supporting the vault meet, and their combined thrust holds them up'.[36] It is only because the pointed arches intersect that the building stands up: the centrifugal forces are essential to its equilibrium.

As a general rule, education tries to get rid of ambivalence. We must love our neighbours and forgive them everything, just as it is morally right to hate our enemies and drive them away. All becomes clear and our controlled ambivalence allows us to express a code of pure interactions: we either love or hate, and we have to choose between the two if we are to be at ease with ourselves.

In an oxymoron, both emotions are essential. And besides, they are inevitable because the wound is a product of history when an external event has inflicted it and imprinted it on the body and the mind. An oxymoron denotes the pathological breaking of a bond that must be forged anew, whereas ambivalence refers to the pathological forming of the bond.

When Baudelaire, who was an expert on oxymorons, writes:

> Each instant eats a piece of the delight
> A man is granted for his earthly season
> . . .
> They are the ore you must refine for gold!

he provides a perfect definition of the alchemy of pain, of the necessary encounter that provokes a metamorphosis in the souls of those who have been badly wounded.[37] They do not have to choose between the pros and the cons, or between the thesis and the antithesis. They have been wounded, and that is all there is to it. All they can do is adapt and be happy, if they can, despite everything. 'O filthy grandeur! O sublime disgrace!'[38]

In a world of 'cold cruelty' it is the poet who is the superman. 'There was one woman I always sat beside. She knew lots of poems,'[39] says Geneviève Anthonioz-de Gaulle in her account of how she was deported to Ravensbrück.[40] She also says: 'Like me, many of my comrades were stronger and more human when they got out of the concentration camps. Others never got out . . . When you are on the point of collapse, a hand stops you from falling. That's how you survive . . . We can be hope's watchmen.'[41]

Poetry and hands that reach out have become dated values in societies that gorge themselves and have gone numb. But for someone who survived Ravensbrück, everything that happened in life referred back to that wound and gave it a quality: are broken bones really worth more than a disabled man? How can you take no notice of poverty when you have licked up the soup that was spilled on the ground? The ordeal becomes the standard by which all things are judged. It is tattooed on the soul, and everything that happens will inevitably refer back to it. For this brave, big-hearted woman, all social acts had to be situated in relation to Ravensbrück: did they afford protection, or did they lead back to Ravensbrück? For those who survived that ordeal, misfortune becomes the evening star that shows the way to the miracle. An oxymoron expresses how suffering can be transformed into a work of art. This is why Jorge Semprun speaks of 'the dazzling misfortunes of life',[42] and why Jean Genet remarks that 'This violence is a calm that disturbs you.'[43] 'Every night, I tell myself a cock-and-bull story to keep myself awake,' explains the nine-year-old Chantal.[44]

Misfortunes are never wonderful. A misfortune is like black, frozen mud or a painful bedsore. It forces us to choose: we can either give in to it or overcome it. Resilience defines the spirit of those who, having suffered a blow, have been able to get over it. The word oxymoron describes the inner world of these wounded victors.

The triumph of the wounded never exonerates the aggressors

Our culture tells us: 'Everything is for the best in the best of worlds.' But people who have survived extreme situations tell us: 'Don't fall for it. The next disaster is on its way. You made me keep quiet when I was suffering in silence because saying it never happened protected you from the truth. You are still trying to protect your own peace of mind by sounding off about the eye-witness accounts of those who survived. You cannot imagine anything that is out of the ordinary. You see anything that deviates from the norm as an act of aggression.'

Telling a victim that it is possible to 'get over it' does not mean relativizing the aggressor's crime. But when the victim's wounds heal and when he or she succeeds in turning the pain into a weapon, the aggressor may look slightly less monstrous. This emotional argument is not unusual. Anyone who presents a paper on resilience gets a virtuously indignant response: 'How dare you say that war is nothing?' someone told the Lebanese speaker who had just explained that lots of children were able to 'get through the war' without too many scars, provided that the adults who were responsible for looking after them did not make their problems worse by talking about their own worries.[45] 'Rest assured that I will never teach my students that raping a woman has no consequences,' said the woman philosophy teacher to the psychiatrist who had just said that women who have been the victims of sexual assaults can still become human beings who are capable of loving and working.[46]

Working on and trying to understand resilience does

not mean that we have to take no notice of those who describe their wounds. Saying that 'some rape victims recover from the trauma quite quickly' really is not the same as saying that we should condone rape.[47] Trying to understand what goes on in the mind of a criminal is not a way of protecting him; it is a way of preventing aggression. It is, however, true to say that, once we understand, we feel less hatred. The courageous Serge Klarsfeld says he does not want to know anything about the personalities of the Nazis he hunts down because, if he formed a personal relationship with them, he could not go on hunting them down.[48] Daniel Herrero, the big-hearted French rugby coach, explains that he does not want his players to talk to their opponents because it would make them less aggressive.

Some people love the hatred that makes them better at what they do. But those whose souls have been wounded do not want to love or hate: they want to survive. All too often the culture that should protect them attacks them in the name of morality: 'I am a fighter. What happened to me [incest] means that I am not like other girls. I've been forced to become wiser and stronger. The programmes on television say that these children turn out badly. I don't want that to happen to me. But it really frightens me,' I was told by a pretty young woman who had just set up her own business and who had to conceal her tragedy in order to appear normal. Having been assaulted by her father, she is now being assaulted by a culture that threatens her with the bleakest of destinies.

If we combine the findings of studies of the population as a whole with those obtained from the 'follow-up of individual cases' we will be in a better position to understand what the law means to a group and what freedom means to the individual.[49] Perhaps then we can allow ourselves to indulge in a little more optimism.

II

Hope Where None Might Be Expected

What makes an impression on a child and stays in his memory means nothing to an adult who is inventing his past

'It's hard, being sentenced to death when you are six years old,' Bernard tells me. 'I was arrested one night. It was the light that woke me up. When the light was suddenly turned on I knew something was going to happen. There were about six men in my bedroom, I think. I was so astonished that I wasn't frightened. It was a small room, and the men were standing around the bed. The ones in plain clothes surprised me, much more so than the soldiers. They were wearing dark glasses, in the middle of the night. Trilbies, and the collars of their fur-lined jackets turned up to make them look good. The German soldiers held back, with their rifles slung over their shoulders.

'When they turned on the light, their revolvers looked ridiculous. Madame Thibault packed a little suitcase and explained to the soldiers that she was prepared to look after me. They told her that they had to arrest me because later, when I was grown up, I would become an enemy of their political party. I was really astonished that they attached so much importance to my future opinions.

'The German soldiers said nothing. They were almost standing to attention. A curious expression on their faces. They stared vaguely at the ceiling, and it was impossible to catch their eye. The French policemen talked among themselves, looked around, took decisions and gave orders. So they were human after all. But the Germans just stood there in the corridor, rifles slung, looking over our heads. They weren't staring into space, but they weren't looking us in the eye either. Not quite so human, if you know what I mean.

'Outside, it was cold and dark. There were a lot more soldiers. The street was blocked by lines of soldiers pointing machine guns at us. They lined up to form a path leading to some lorries with tarpaulins over them and some black cars. On the pavement, the wicked soldiers were shouting and kicking people. In the car they'd pushed me into, a man was crying, looking straight ahead. I felt no pain, no fear. Just really astonished because, when he swallowed his saliva, the weeping man's Adam's apple bobbed up and down.'

The human memory is so constructed that an event that is devoid of meaning leaves no trace. In the world of a child, being surprised by the sight of an Adam's apple leaves a bolder trace than the prospect of imminent death. The word 'death' has yet to become an adult word, whereas an Adam's apple that is bobbing up and down leaves a lasting impression. For a child, that is a powerful emotion.

Adults invent their past because they think but

cannot see, whereas the memory of a child, which is impressed by men wearing dark glasses at night, is more specific than that of adults, who are deceived by their own theories. Their memories simply do not retain the same things.

The memory of adults becomes richer as they grow older thanks to the social reconstructions that give the event a meaning, whereas a child's memory recalls details that mean something to him. The dark glasses tell the child that adults are capable of being illogical. And the bobbing Adam's apple reveals an unexpectedly sexual note. The German soldiers and the French policemen do not become part of the child's memory until fifty years later, in a different social context that demands the truth.

We must not, however, denigrate retrospective memories too much. They are not lies, but reconstructions of the past. The narrative is obviously shaped by the intentions of the speaker and the impression the speaker wants to make on the person he or she is addressing. In order to influence them, events from the past are used to invent an autobiographical chimera. Every element in it is true, and yet its sole function is to create an animal that exists only in the story being constructed.

This highly contextualized memory depends on how the questions are asked. If we ask 'How many football matches did you see during the last World Cup?' we will get only vague answers. If we ask 'Did you see that match?' the answers will be much more specific. The social context gives autobiographical memories more reliable markers than a sequence of events. We are designed to see the outside world as something that is self-evident, as an image that is stamped on our memory, and which we later try to locate in a setting of family or other social points of reference. It is those external points of reference that give the sequence of inner images their coherence. If they do not, our memories pile up in the form of tangled images, and it is very difficult for any meaning to emerge.

These muddled images can only be organized into a temporal sequence if someone else can date what has happened to us. Children in institutional care who have been moved on twenty or thirty times within the space of ten years retain memories that are specific but completely incoherent. They will describe how a supervisor addressed them with only brief hand signals or by clicking his tongue so that he would not have to speak to them. They remember the colour of the leaves, the shape of the secret den they built, or playing jacks as they sprawled in the dust, but they cannot say where, why or how these specific scenes took place. A moment that is devoid of meaning lingers in their memories, like a photo taken with a flash. Wordless stories are imprinted on their memories because they triggered an emotional response, but they are meaningless to adults, even though they were involved in the same events. Images make no sense if they cannot be situated and turned into a narrative.

The memory-image of an Adam's apple makes a strong impression on a child who has been sentenced to death, but it escapes the attention of adults. As for wearing dark glasses at night, an adult finds this hard to believe. And yet, fifty years later, the eye-witness accounts of some of the people who made those arrests confirm that some French detectives did wear dark glasses to hide their eyes.

It is the emotion we feel at the time that explains why certain events are transformed into memories whilst others leave no trace. And the child's anecdotal history does as much as history itself to explain the emotion.[1]

When President Kennedy was killed, I was spending the day with my wife's family. I think I recall hearing the news on the radio, but I am not sure, whereas the images of the furniture in our bedroom, of the counterpane on the bed, and even of what the weather was like as I walked across the garden to tell my family what had happened are still so clear that I could describe them in detail. On the other hand, I found it impossible to tell whether all this took place in Paris or in Montpellier.

The murder of a president means nothing to a small child. A child's representational space is still too close at hand to be affected by an event that takes place far away. The emotional responses of the adults the child loves do, on the other hand, create a world that he or she can experience. The emotions displayed by the child's attachment figures therefore act as markers that fix his memory-images. Those emotions fix events in the form of memories and make them coherent, provided that the child encounters someone who can turn them into a story.

During the London Blitz, children felt safe when their mothers were confident, just as Mr Human Bomb's little hostages laughed when their teacher turned it all into a game

Anna Freud noted how calm the infants were in air-raid shelters during Luftwaffe raids on London in the Second World War. Bombs whistled around them, the earth shook and the walls of the shelter quaked, but that had no effect on them. The explanation is simple, she remarked: their world had not changed. They were still safe in their mothers' arms. If its mother's mind is at rest, the infant feels perfectly safe in her arms. But if the mother trembles or simply becomes tense, the baby's world is turned upside down. Subsequently, or when speech has brought about a transformation in the child's world, he will still be immersed in the emotions of others. But it is the narrative that will freeze the images and give them a meaning.

When 'Mr Human Bomb' took them hostage at the nursery school in Neuilly-sur-Seine, the children were more frightened of the people who saved them than of the man who was threatening their lives.[2] In the adult world, the threat was posed by a man who was strapped with grenades and threatening to blow up both himself and the children. In the children's world, the man was not frightening. His presence was a curious incident, with lots of unusual comings and goings and unexpected games. Especially as their teacher was clever enough to discover the defence mechanism illustrated by Roberto Benigni in *La Vita è bella* and told them that the man was playing a game. When, on the other hand, the police burst into the school and grabbed some of the little ones in an attempt to rescue them, the children thought they were being taken away from 'safety' by hooded thieves who were running away as fast as they could with the little bodies in their arms. They were running through a crowd of adults who were shouting at them to tell them how to reach safety. That was the real horror.[3] There was a real danger that it would imprint specific images on their memories. Perhaps the sound of running feet. Perhaps the sound of a badge jingling on a leather jerkin. Perhaps an unshaven cheek. A single detail can be all it takes to symbolize horror, unless the emotion is reworked, through either a drawing, a play, a story or anything else that can transform the effect. If the children are left alone, the memory of how frightened they were will come back to them every night in the form of a working drawing. Because it has been stylized, the memory will give everyday objects the power to evoke their fear. But if the children can address their drawings, stories, thoughts or playlets to someone who laughs at them, makes comments about them or bursts into tears, they can control their emotions because they can, thanks to their little creations, shape their images, words and gestures in such a way that they influence others. It is the presence of the spectator that allows the children to get a new grip on themselves.

For five-year-old Michel, being arrested was like going to a party because he had suffered from emotional isolation before being interned in Drancy; but, even today, Renate, who adored her mother, still sees her body: she was shot during the liberation of France

Little Michel, who was five, spent three weeks interned in the Drancy camp during the Second World War.[4] He then succeeded in escaping during a transfer. Before being arrested, he had spent six months in the comfortable room where he had been hidden by a Parisian family. Those six months were spent in almost complete social and sensory isolation: no radio, nothing to read, no friends, no family. The generous people who brought him his meals spoke to him twice a day. After a few weeks of isolation, the child eventually stopped answering them. After the first month of isolation, all he did was walk round and round the table. He repeated the action so many times that it became stereotypical; he took big strides and swung his arms in a pendulum movement. Sometimes, he would stop walking and either rock backwards and forwards or spin like a top. When these internal stimuli made him dizzy, he would lie on the floor and lick his knees.

He did not say a word when he was arrested.

For Michel, being interned was a resurrection. He rediscovered life and the noises, faces and the rhythm of meals and encounters he had forgotten during his long period of solitude. He was eager to see new faces. The arrival of every new batch of prisoners was a fascinating event. Meeting other children was extremely emotional, especially as they smiled at each other, talked to each other and played together.

Fifty years later, Michel and the family who had hidden him compared memories. The results were astonishing. The brave Parisians who had saved the child's life had no idea of the suffering he had endured in their care. When they were asked specific questions about what they recalled, the adults remembered only the child's stereotypical behaviour and silence. For them, it was the social context of what had gone on around them that was significant: the day the neighbour who used to bring the can of milk heard footsteps and wanted to know what was going on in the lounge . . . the day the police came to look around the house but forgot about that room . . . the day the child ran away despite all their warnings, and put the lives of the family in danger.

As he listened to these stories, a few images came back to Michel. He had no social memories: he remembered nothing about the neighbour or the detectives, and nothing about running away. He remembered a few things: a table mat, a small clock, licking his knees. He was horrified to learn that he had spent six months in that room, because those units of time existed only in the minds of the adults, who had retained their social markers, and not in his mind.

It was only after this affectionate exchange that Michel dared to tell us that being interned in Drancy had been like going to a party. He came back to life and underwent a resurrection. He said that more harm had probably been done to him by the sensory isolation inflicted on him by the family who saved his life than by the internment that sentenced him to death.

Renate was not so lucky when France was liberated in 1945. She was five when she saw her father being arrested by a jubilant group of young men carrying guns and wearing armbands. She was a bit frightened but did not suffer too much because she was not very attached to him; he had made only brief appearances in her life. When, on the other hand, her mother was tried before a court conducted from a trestle table in the village square, she realized that something very serious was about to happen. That is why she ran to where she heard the shots coming from. She pushed through the legs of the adults only to see the body of her mother lying on the ground. At that moment two images were imprinted on her for the rest of her life. That of her mother who had been shot in the stomach. And of a man's voice simply telling the little girl: 'She was calling for you only a moment ago.' When the coffin containing her mother was being lowered into the grave, Renate picked up a piece of the rope supporting the coffin. Renate has been living with that memory for over fifty years. As soon as she relaxes or drops her guard, the image of a bullet-holed dress suddenly appears in her inner world: 'Why, why there? . . .' And in her memory, what the man said – 'She was calling for you only a moment ago' – has, after the event, come to mean 'You didn't even say goodbye to her.' So Renate consoles herself with the piece of rope, which was something that had been close to her mother but had not passed judgement on her. She keeps the rope in a box on the mantelpiece and often looks at it. She was five, so how was she to understand that her father was one of

Doriot's bodyguards?[5] She was just a little girl, so how could she understand that a woman who had married a man like that and who kept house in the fine home of a collaborator deserved to die. Her mother was beautiful and cheerful. Why shoot her in the stomach?

Renate was afterwards brought up in a very harsh religious institution where, because of her family history, no one ever spoke to her. She is now a social worker in the Nice area, which she has never left. The painful memories of the man's words and the image of her dead mother faded during the years after she married and had children. When her children left home, Renate discovered that her memories had merely been buried and came back to her every night, as though it had happened yesterday.

Perhaps Renate might have suffered less if she had been able to talk about what happened, turn it into a drawing, a book or a work of art, or even been active in one of the associations of children whose parents had been shot at liberation. But the culture of the day would never have allowed her to do that: a culture tolerates only those historical accounts that reinforce its own myth.

The emotion that freezes memories is a product of an encounter between the child's level of development and its external markers.

We are not responsive to the same information at all ages: an infant who lives in his mother's arms knows nothing about presidents. A girl cannot understand the political reasons why her mother was shot. It is not the objective nature of the situation that affects us most. Hunger, cold and attack obviously do play a role because they are immediate stimuli that make us want to eat, warm ourselves up or try to protect ourselves. But our mental world is shaped by our representations and the markers that structure our inner world. That is why family events such as a quarrel between our parents, their rituals as a couple, or moving house stir up emotions that date our memories. Subsequently, or as we grow up, our markers become even more social: school, teachers, playground fights and exams, and then changes of job and political events, organize the environment that penetrates us and permeates our subjective world.

That is why the meaning we attribute to events is for private use only, even though it is dated by external factors. But as soon as we begin to turn them into stories, our memories cease to be meaningless: 'So I was twenty, and one day, it was two in the afternoon and I remember it perfectly, I flung myself on a sofa in the presence of my mother and said: "I can't take any more." My mother replied: "If I'd known, I'd have had an abortion." That made an extraordinary impression on me, but it was not entirely negative. Rather than being appalled, I remember giving a sort of smile, and it was like a revelation: being the product of chance and not of some necessity was in a way a liberation,' recalls the Romanian-born essayist Emil Michel Cioran.[6]

If we were creatures of logic, our sufferings would be endless. But given that we are psychological beings, we give every event a private meaning that has been imprinted on us by our environment in the course of our development and history. Which explains why some people can be shattered by hearing something like that, whilst others feel liberated.

For young Michel, being interned in Drancy was like going to a party because, in the course of his history, he had previously experienced a period of terrible sensory deprivation that probably damaged those parts of the brain that control emotions and memories. For him, being interned in the camp meant entering a wonderfully warm environment. He was eager to be confronted by the slightest human contact because, for him, it meant that he was coming back to life; for others, it was a death sentence.

When the real world is terrifying, daydreams can give rise to insane hopes; in Auschwitz or during the war in the Pacific, it was the poet who was a superman

The example of Michel explains the astonishing variations in the way different people respond to the same aggression. In the same camp and at the same time were three children who had been arrested along with their mother. One morning she was separated from them and disappeared. She was probably taken to Auschwitz. When Albert, who was ten, realized that they would never see her again, his immediate reaction was to think, 'Right, I'll have to get by on my own now.' He found a shelter for his brother and his little sister. And then he went off to find them something to eat. Edouard, who was the eldest, was in total despair. Withdrawing into himself, he could think of nothing but his mother, the emptiness and the immense void that her sudden disappearance would leave inside him for the rest of his life. As for little Rose, who was the youngest, she is amazed by the hatred she still feels for the mother who disappeared and still cannot stop herself thinking, 'Mum, I hate you because you abandoned us.'

After the war Albert was placed in a foster family that showed him no kindness. He worked terribly hard, getting up at four to do the housework before he went to school. The fact that there was no kindness did not mean that there were no sexual advances. His foster mother made advances on two or three occasions, and then gave up trying. For his part, the foster father tried to force himself on the boy, who fought back vigorously. Nothing more was said about these incidents. After these mercifully unsuccessful advances, Albert felt a strange sensation. He was amazed at how calm he felt inside, because the assaults allowed him to think to himself: 'That's that. I want nothing more to do with these people. They've given me a home. I do their housework. We're quits. I'll leave as soon as I'm old enough.' His foster parents' assaults had set Albert free in the same way that the admission 'If I'd known, I'd have had an abortion' set Cioran free. It is the social and temporal context that explains these unexpected reactions, which are more common than one might think. Just as little Michel experienced his internment in Drancy as a kind of party because of his previous isolation, Albert made psychological use of the assaults in order to set himself free because, were it not for them, he would have felt he owed his foster family something and would have worked for them until he became depersonalized.

This type of contextual reasoning sheds some light on the mystery of why people react to traumas in different ways. We can establish a sort of scale to measure degrees of stress. At a very general level, it is quite accurate. If we attempt to evaluate the levels of stress produced by life's ordeals in universal terms, our scale rates stress caused by the death of a partner as a maximum 100.[7] Getting divorced, even by consent, is roughly equivalent to being put in prison – or getting married. Retirement is also high on the stress scale. It is more stressful than falling into debt or losing one's job. Even though they are at the very bottom of the scale, the stress involved in holidays, Christmas and fines still merit a score of 10. But what the scale does not tell us is that the worst form of stress is an absence of stress, because the feeling that there is no life before death gives rise to a despairing feeling of emptiness in the face of the void.

In order to understand resilience, which is an internal mechanism that allows us to cope with life's adversities, we have to look at those who do not conform to this scale. Surviving an ordeal can sometimes reveal an emotional capability that we cannot admit to. 'When I realized that my mother was going to die, my anxiety vanished,' I was told by a young man who had previously been terrified by the overpowering presence of that dazzling woman. On the other hand, horror can sometimes place a new emphasis on tenderness. Certain adolescents who have been numbed because they have been overprotected discover this peculiar form of eroticization. 'When you tell me that having since 1968 been in the thick of the most horrible events in the world was probably too much for me, let me reassure you that, whilst I may have lost some illusions, I feel a greater tenderness,' the photographer Michel Laurent wrote to his wife when he came back from Vietnam.[8]

When the real world is terrifying, daydreams can give rise to insane hopes that make it bearable:

Back to the camp back to the ruck ...
Life will be beautiful when freedom comes ...
We'll just have to live
what could be simpler ...
for those who know
how to suffer how to die?
...
Stop grumbling
that's life
what did you dream of over there?[9]

Those who want for nothing think that poetry is outmoded, but it becomes something that allows us to survive when the real world is unbearable.

As a young man, Sidney Stewart fought in the Pacific during the Second World War. When he was taken prisoner by the Japanese in the hell of the Philippines jungle, he was astonished to see that the first to die were the most muscular American footballers. Superman can only live in a cocoon. In order to train, he must eat well, sleep well, take his vitamins and think of nothing else. In a context of unspeakable violence in which rain, heat, animals and men are fighting to see who can be the most cruel, it is the man who can retreat into his own inner world who is best able to resist. At such times, poets become supermen. They can take shelter in an immaterial world where they meet artists, philosophers, mystics and all those who are able to live in a transcendental element. They revel in their astonishment at surviving, and are eager to know why. That is how they escape the cruelty of the place they are in. Their inner representations sometimes allow them to experience a great feeling of beauty, even though the real world around them is dreadful.

We need categories: classifying, delineating and separating can help us to think by shaping the objects that we imbue with certain qualities. We see the world more clearly when we have conceptualized it in this way. Categories can also be misleading. Pure objects exist only in the realm of ideas. It is we who put the world into categories. In the real world, everything is muddled up together. At his darkest moment, when death is imminent, Rass, the young American from the USS *Watonga*, discovers to his astonishment the delights of prayer, and experiences the luxury of life: 'When I see those guys die, I think "Well, life's a luxury"'.[10]

It has often been noted that, in extreme situations, conflicting emotions are closely related. It is at the point when we are in danger of losing it that we discover with delight our attachment to the object which, now that it has been aroused by that discovery, allows us to snuggle up to an individual who, an hour earlier, left us indifferent. Survivors describe their astonishing feeling of being under a death sentence.

Living on borrowed time gives them a facetious cheerfulness. When you have come face to face with death, nothing is banal. It is because they want to feel that sensation that gamblers bet against impossible odds that make it almost inevitable that they will lose. If they do win, they squander the money they never expected to have.

Rather than posing the problem in terms of a single cause with measurable effects, the notion of resilience represents an attempt to understand how, when we are hit, we can roll with the punches, react in various ways or even bounce back. It may well be true that the experience of sexual dysfunctionality is equivalent to 40 units on our 100-unit scale of stress at the level of the population as a whole, but the same is not necessarily true at the individual level. I know one young man who, after finding himself to be impotent on only one occasion, was flooded with such anxiety that his whole life was thrown into turmoil. But I also know a young woman – with a great interest in sex, as it happens – who, after one unsatisfactory encounter, experienced an astonishing feeling of liberation. For the boy, the failure meant 'I will never have a family, and I need one so badly.' For the girl, the same difficult moment meant 'This is the man for me. If we do become a couple, I will love him so much that it is very likely that I'll have him on a string and become depersonalized, as I already have done. My anxiety about loving stops me feeling any pleasure and is taking away part of my personality. That failure has given me back my freedom. That's why I only reach orgasm when I'm with men I don't love.' If we look at our stress scale and add together the boy's level of stress (an estimated 60) and the girl's (about 20), the statistics tell us that, at the level of the population as a whole, the experience of impotence is equivalent to 40 units of stress, even though the two individuals concerned experienced very different emotions.

It would be more accurate to say that resilience is both a diachronic and a synchronic process. Biological and developmental forces are articulated with a social context to create a self-representation that allows the subject to see his or her life in historical terms.

To put it more simply, resilience is a sweater knitted from developmental, emotional and social strands of wool. That is why it is more helpful to describe the history of a resilient personality. We can then try to understand how it dodges the strokes of fate and still contrives to use solid supports in order to knit itself.

Resilience is a mesh and not a substance. We are forced to knit ourselves, using the people and things we meet in our emotional and social environments. And when it is all over and we can look back at our lives from heaven, we say to ourselves: 'The things I've been through. I've come one hell of a long way. It wasn't always an easy journey.'

*We are wanderers, but we do have a sense
of direction; even when we know where we
come from, the genetics can be imaginary;
and when we know nothing about our past,
we can invent it at our leisure*

'We are wanderers, but we do have a sense of direction.'[1] We are not inevitably destined to be thrown completely off course by strokes of fate. When we know where we are going we experience nothing more than some minor turbulence. Whatever our origins, whatever the colour of our skin and whether or not we have a family, we are doomed to wander. Our destiny is shaped like a safety pin. Whilst we are on the upward curve, or during our early childhood, we identify with those we are born of, irrespective of whether we actually know them or have just imagined them. We negotiate the bend in the safety pin during our adolescence, when we all have to prohibit incest in order to become part of human society. We then have to leave the people we love and court those we will love in a different way. The bend in the safety pin directs us towards the family we will try to create to make our dreams come true.

Our line of descent is the solid part of the plinth on which our identity is constructed. The bend in the pin would appear to be the taboo on incest. This is the linchpin that obliges us to leave the order into which we are inserted by our line of descent and to experiment with the new order we create when we marry. In this way, culture avoids the dangers of both an order that petrifies and a disorder that pulverizes.

Those whose memories play tricks on them surrender to the delights of the trials and tribulations of the past: 'In my family, *monsieur*, we shed our blood for the French nation,' I was told by a small gentleman who was both pink and plump, and who took great pleasure in imagining how such a tragic past could have helped to make him what he was!

Another man said to me by way of introduction: 'One of my ancestors took up arms against Pope Julius II.' As I looked at him, I thought to myself that a study of genetics would disappoint him because marriage meant something very different in the sixteenth century. As for the factors that influence impregnation, they are so mysterious that such a line of descent cannot be based on anything but an imaginary biology.

And yet, an untruth can be effective and can shape our sense of selfhood. A supra-individual identification with the soldiers of Louis XIV or with the man who stood up to Julius II fills the inner world of their descendents with glorious men. It creates an impression of glory, a sort of sentimental cascade that apparently flows down the generations. An imaginary genetics makes those who believe in it feel at ease with themselves. It organizes a behavioural code and a way of expressing emotions that correspond to this image: a man who is descended from a man who stood up to Julius II acts decisively. He has forthright opinions and is condescending towards others. All the more so in that his imaginary genetics feeds on family and social stories, a few heirlooms and two or three myths that have been passed on from one generation to the next.

In some cases, an imaginary genetics composes a story that becomes a social constraint: 'I am descended from generations of shopkeepers. We don't waste our time going to school or university.' We also hear it said that: 'In our family, we commit suicide at the age of about thirty,' and what is no more than a mythical prophecy creates anxious feelings about the future.

Orphans always remember their parents as they were when they were young; when they are forced to become independent and become prisoners of freedom, they always find treasures that lend an enchantment to their desolate reality

Children who have no line of descent or no parents do not enjoy the benefits of this facile identification. They therefore win the freedom to invent both their future and their past: 'A father would have ballasted me with a few lasting prejudices; creating my principles from his words, my knowledge from his ignorance, my pride from his rancour, and my laws from his manias, he would have dwelt in me ... My begetter would have decided on my future ... Land and a house give a young heir a stable image of himself ... I was no one's master and nothing belonged to me.'[12] The fact that Jean-Paul Sartre was not 'the perpetuator-to-be of my father's work' gave him his freedom by taking away his soul. A soul is the red thread which, in the British Royal Navy, guarantees that the twist in a rope is continuous. In Sartre's case, having no soul meant being forced to be independent, being condemned to be free.

It is only the dead who never die. When a child is old enough to have some idea of what death means, she understands that the lives of her parents are destined to end with a full stop. She learns to love parents who are growing older and weaker. She learns to tolerate the fact that those closest to her can be wrong and can be unfair. The same is never true of orphans, whose parents remain forever young in their memories. Some clue, such as a photo or the stories told by someone who 'knew your father well: he was tall and very cheerful', allows the image of an active, amiable man, or a mother who was always beautiful and easy to love, to live on in their inner world. Hence the great paradox: a child with a family basks in the affection of parents who are not perfect, whereas a child with 'no family' is faced with a categorical choice between a parental void that forces him to be free and the emotional substitute who provides him with support and stability. His life oscillates between the wanderings that give him an intoxicating but anxiety-ridden freedom, and a search for the support that strengthens and imprisons him.

When she lost her parents, Géraldine found that she did not have the support that would have allowed her to undertake the process of mourning. Having no parents and no support, she had no option but to renounce all forms of love. On the other hand, she was completely free and had no ties, and could therefore decide what to do purely on the basis of whatever came into her head.[13] Anyone who has had dealings with street children or children orphaned at an early age is familiar with the impression of maturity given by youngsters who have been forced to look after themselves in the way that an adult would look after them. But the impression is deceptive. A child with a family expects to be given a structure, and then rebels against those who impose it. Because he has been imbued with another person's soul, he can inscribe himself into a culture and a line of descent. A child with no family, on the other hand, has to use splitting mechanisms to adapt to a threatening outside world. The sociable part of her personality is confronted with a desolate reality. She has nothing. She has no home.

Street children sleep wherever they can: on a grating, in a doorway or huddled together for warmth. Children without families move from institution to institution, sometimes sleep in beds provided by foster families they do not know, and sometimes sleep on bales of straw in a barn, as did many who were taken into care after the war. But the cryptic part of her inner world is filled with nothing but pain. Every night, she imagines she is with her parents, who never die.

In the real world, children like this grow up too quickly, but the parents who live on inside their heads remain young, good looking, cheerful and warm. They kiss her goodnight every night. In a real world in which wandering can be a desolate experience, the child sees poetic signs that only she can understand. Georges Perec admits: 'I have no memory of my father other than the one about the key or coin he might have given me one evening on his return from work.'[14] In other words, 'Because you have a family, you just see an ordinary key. But because I have lost both my parents, I know that there is something magical about that key. And besides, it could be either a key or a coin, I can't really remember. But it was my father's. So there must be something precious about it that gives me strength, gives me hope.'

All children without families have treasures like this. In what can sometimes be forbidding institutions, they hide their treasures under the mattress, close to their heads so that they can be even closer to them. But do not make the mistake of thinking that it is just a piece of rope or a scrap of newspaper that has turned yellow: it is a talisman. 'This piece of rope represents strength and love because it touched my mother's coffin after she was shot in the stomach . . . That grubby scrap of newspaper is precious because I think it's about my father. He was a brave soldier, killed in battle. I can't read, but something tells me that a magical power that's invisible to adults says good things about my father in that yellowed paper.'

From an adult point of view, these children have grown up too quickly and are wandering through a desolate world: nowhere to live, nowhere to sleep, nothing to eat and no school to go to. But because they look too closely at the real world, adults fail to see the magical powers of a piece of rope or a torn scrap of newspaper. And so, acting in the name of hygiene and the rules, they throw away these pathetic treasures and smash up the crypts and the enchanted tunnels where these damaged children take refuge on their wanderings and where they are reunited with the parents they have lost. That is why destroying their little treasures and their imaginary crypts always makes them run away for good.

If we really wish to support these damaged children, we have to help them to become active, and not give them everything they ask for. Giving them more and more will not help them, but asking more of them can make them stronger.

Exiles are orphans too: they will get over their loss if the culture that takes them in supports the wounded; for their children, school and work become happy places that heal the parent's wound

The experience of exile allows us to understand the extent to which neediness is a protective factor. Virtually all studies prove that all migrants suffer from some form of anxiety. They have been cut off from their roots. They have to live and breathe in a linguistic environment that they do not understand. Even a minor social encounter leaves them helpless because they cannot understand the words and gestures that might otherwise help them to orientate themselves. Worst of all, they have been separated from their families. Almost all their bonds have been severed. The lonelier a migrant feels, the more anxious he will become. As a result, they take more medication than the population at large, and are more likely to be involved in criminal activity.[15] A child responds to social violence by using splitting mechanisms to make it bearable, but the personal identity of a migrant is shattered when the social body surrounding him becomes incoherent, when ties are loosened and when events lose their meaning.

The explanation for the euphoria of the first months is probably a phenomenon similar to that experienced by little Michel. He was deliriously happy when he was interned in Drancy because he had previously suffered the torment of severe social isolation. Such people leave their countries of origin because they are unhappy there, and because dreaming of the host country allows them to entertain extravagant hopes.

Even if they find it incomprehensible, it takes only one meeting or one event to convince them that they are beginning to live out their dreams in the real world. But the honeymoon lasts for only a few months, and coming back to earth is a painful experience. It is now that the anxieties and the acts of desperation begin. Three factors have a great impact on the way migrants adapt: the welcome they receive, the meaning of that welcome, and their gender. A migrant who changes cultures but brings a piece of his world of origin with him is much less disoriented because he still has a few markers from the past around him. These factors help him to find his way around the host culture more quickly.

The Vietnamese boat people who were dispersed to the south of France were welcomed by similar families who spoke their language and who had preserved a few customs. A welcome structure was immediately organized to give them financial assistance, to find housing for them, to teach them French and to find them jobs. Within the space of a few years their children were going to school, fishing for rainbow wrasse and speaking with Marseillais accents. Part of the same population, which had suffered terrible violence in Vietnam, was dispersed to Britain, where there was no structure to welcome them. In that small group, consumption of medication was extremely high, as was the rate of delinquency. The small cohort of children who were placed in hostels had a very high incidence of psychiatric disorders, which disappeared as soon as they were adopted.[16]

Two extreme social strategies appear to have the most adverse effects on these populations: isolation and assimilation. In Winnipeg, a relatively isolated town in the middle of the Canadian prairies, there is a colony of Ethiopian refugees which numbers only around 200 individuals.[17] The colony suffered greatly as a result of its isolation, which was to the group what sensory deprivation is to an individual: the refugees found it impossible to get out and about or to turn to those around them for support. Both Haitian refugees and Hassidic Jewish communities exemplify the difficulties that arise when groups distance themselves from other cultural worlds. The men marry only when they are forced to do so. They are poorly socialized and experience psychiatric problems.

Yet assimilation appears to be just as bad. It is based

upon a social contract with the migrants: become like us and forget about your own past. Only then will we welcome you. Because it deprives them of their old identity, this unwritten contract places migrants at the mercy of the environment in which they find themselves. They become ghosts reliant upon welfare. The effect of amputating their history is a collective equivalent to repression. We sometimes see an unexpected explosion of violent behaviour in a group thought to have assimilated peacefully. All too often it is forgotten that repression does less damage than the return of the repressed.[18] The group appears to have been assimilated because it has scotomized part of reality – created a blind spot to prevent itself seeing certain problems or working them through by con-fronting them in both verbal and social terms. That is the price paid for assimilation. The host culture also has to pay a very high price in order to assimilate human beings who have had part of their identity amputated. Eventually, some very minor event will block the safety valve and the problem will explode, much to the surprise of all concerned.

A third option, biculturalism, is not the easiest of solutions, as it requires the migrants to live in two different mental worlds. It does, however, appear to be more humane and richer than the other two.[19] The stress of acculturation is reduced because the migrants are given some support. Their feeling of security acts as a base camp that allows them to explore and learn about the host culture. Bilingual Mexicans living in the southern United States have almost three times fewer medical problems than those who speak no English. Those Korean Canadians who speak only their birth language are the most marginalized and suffer the highest levels of stress. When parents speak only their language of origin and when children speak only the language of the host country, the linguistic divide causes splits within the family as one generation cannot understand the next. This is very unfair all round because, in almost all cases, the parents' reluctance to teach their children their language of origin is motivated by a desire to ensure that their offspring will assimilate more quickly.

Gender also plays an important role in the psychotrauma of exile. Women are less likely to emigrate, but their sufferings are greater when they are on their own. It is usually the men who interact with host-country colleagues in the workplace, and so integrate more quickly than women (or retirees) who stay at home. Those who stay at home often form groups that stoke a nostalgia for the country they have lost.

The painful cultural wrench of being torn away from one's origins does not, however, always have harmful effects. For the children of immigrants, school can become a place where they can fight for their integration. When their children do well at school, it has a reparative effect on immigrant parents. Local children, in contrast, all too often find school boring because it does not have the meaning it had for their parents. Armenian children had to learn to speak French better than anyone else in the class in order to reassure their parents. And in the Jewish families who were driven out of central Europe, one phrase recurs like a triumphant refrain: 'My son has become his boss's right-hand man.' Achievement restores his parents' pride. For all these reasons, it is not unusual for new arrivals to reach quickly levels of mental health similar to or better than those of the local population. When later arrivals are given support, they succeed in overcoming their ordeals to such an extent that their children sometimes do better at school than those who arrived before them. As for levels of delinquency, they vary enormously from one group to another and are basically determined by opportunities to integrate.[20]

A survivor is a hero who is guilty of having killed death

Most of the factors that make a child resilient are to be found in his environment. A child's genetic make-up might have a bearing on his physical health, but at a very early stage in his development a second part of his ability to survive is imprinted on him by his emotional environment. Most of the factors that determine an individual's resistance are in fact knitted around him by the psychosocial structures which signpost the path through the brain's circuitry that will allow him to blossom. Even his inner world is a product of these three elements. This form of argument is illustrated by the stories of children who have survived a close encounter with death.

Children are not usually 'survivors'. They are living beings whose mental worlds are fully populated simply because they are blossoming and learning to live. It is only adults who apply the term 'survivor', for example to a newborn daughter who almost died of toxicosis and is alive only because she was rehydrated; the baby has no awareness of how close she came to death. By the time the girl is six, however, she has some idea of what death means, and can understand that she almost died at birth. From that point onwards the 'survivor' representation will be imprinted on her mind.

This situation is not unusual. It allows us to understand how a real event (such as war or famine) that takes place in the outside world inscribes an emotional trace in the child's inner world. The way others see that trace gives it a meaning, and it then shapes an inner feeling of selfhood: 'I am the boy who survived.'

Once a child understands that he has had a close encounter with death, there is a to-and-fro movement between his inner world and what is going on around him when the social discourse that says 'He's a hero' imbues his mental world with the feeling that he is someone out of the ordinary.

What astonishes us as children is not the fact that we are alive, and still less the fact that we have survived. It is the wonder of the outside world that fascinates us and lends enchantment to our inner world. Soap bubbles floating through the air or petals falling from a rose bush are real events. They take place in the outside world but they are still exhilarating.

The notion of survival implies that the child thinks he almost lost this world and ceased to be part of it. Such a representation requires an advanced degree of personalization, and a mental life capable of imagining the void, the infinite and the absolute. It is as though the child were thinking: 'An imperious force almost took me away from this wonder. But the fact that I have escaped the all-powerful force that will later be known as death means that I am stronger than death.' It is as though there had been a battle and the child himself had killed death. 'The moment of survival is the moment of power.'[21] This feeling, which is frequently experienced by survivors, is deeply ambivalent. I have killed death, Canetti tells us. I have killed death because I have survived. The very fact that I am here proves that I am stronger than death. Our words define unalloyed feelings but, deep down inside, we always have mixed feelings. The guilt of survivors is always tinged with megalomania. 'All grief is insignificant measured against this elemental triumph.'[22] For someone who has lived through the exhilarating moment of having killed death, the miseries of daily life look quite laughable. Many survivors therefore display a morbid courage: 'This pain means nothing to a terrified conqueror like me. When you have been lucky enough to be stronger than death, you really can't allow yourself to be defeated by some pathetic adversity. I have nothing to eat tonight, the walls of my bedroom are covered in hoar frost, I'm shivering with cold as I lie in bed, and I have to get up at four to wash the floor before rushing out to school. So what? I'm already an old man at fifteen, and I've known worse.' This is not an attempt to eroticize suffering; the pain is real, it hurts and it never stops, but it provokes defiance and not groans. Any challenge comes to look like an ordeal: if I win again, if the judgement of God grants me victory, if I survive my ordeal at the hand of the natural elements, ordeals by water and fire, if I can be stronger than hunger, cold and social hostility, I can prove to myself that I have the right to live even though I am guilty. But this fight is fought on a knife edge. If by some misfortune I lose, that will prove that they were quite right to try to kill me.

This inner world of mixed feelings explains why survivors seem so paradoxical to outside observers. Even though it was won at great cost, their victory gives them a strange inner serenity. Witnesses say, 'He's extraordinarily well balanced, considering everything he's been through.' Those who believe that human beings form a hierarchy will explain that it is their 'higher qualities' that make survivors so calm. Such arguments are total nonsense because, if the survivor had failed, he would have shown just how vulnerable he is. Even in the most desperate situations he believes that he will win because he has already been given the opportunity to triumph over death. Should he fail, however, he accepts that his killers are right and he succumbs to a melancholic guilt. Because he is forced to win in order to experience some peace, any failure awakens the empty feeling that he deserved to die.

In the event of failure, someone who is not a survivor is disappointed. And then, after a while, he puts his energies into something else. His scars heal and he develops a new project. He even finds excuses that allow him to live with his failure: 'She really wasn't the woman for me. Fortunately, she left me.' But the survivor's failure eventually proves to him that he deserved to die: 'I don't have the right to live. I deserved to die; much more so than my parents, who were killed at my side. They should have lived, and not me.' Any failure becomes a defeat that releases the buried guilt: 'My parents told me not to talk to the Shining Path soldiers. One day when I was five, my ball rolled in their direction and they played football with me. Shortly afterwards, my parents were shot. Until I was twenty, I thought that, without realizing it, I must have let the soldiers know that my parents hated them by playing with them. When I disobeyed my parents, I sentenced them to death.'

Survivors feel guilty, which explains why they behave as though they are atoning. People who see them from the outside speak of their 'generosity' or 'austerity'. Oblation at one's own expense is in fact a good bargain; it takes away our feeling of guilt. Depriving ourselves for the sake of others makes us stop feeling like criminals. We did not really kill our parents, and we become the bringers of good luck. The behaviour that ruins us changes our sense of selfhood, and transforms a guilty party into a generous donor.

Child psychologist Bruno Bettelheim, himself a refugee from Nazism, knew all about survivor guilt, but he saw it as a simple misery when it is in fact a compound misery. There is the pride of a man who has shown himself to be stronger than death, the obligation to succeed on a knife edge, and the astonishing serenity that comes from self-surrender. Bettelheim could not experience this feeling of compound misery because he suffered constant depression long before he was deported to Dachau.[23]

Throughout his life he experienced nothing but sadness, not that it prevented him from becoming resilient. The concept of resilience refers to the mechanism that allows us to bounce back when fate knocks us down, and not to a talent for happiness.

A love of death can even be a way of defending ourselves from our fear of dying. That is precisely what melancholics do. The theatricality of death is the only thing that gives them any peace. 'Funerals are the only things that make me feel at ease with myself. When everyone is crying, I no longer feel like a monster because I have lost the will to live. I'm just like everyone else. It gives me such a feeling of peace that just coming into contact with me soothes the family's pain.' The other classic example is that of melancholics who explain that it is only by preparing to commit suicide that they can experience some peace in their pain-filled lives: 'As soon as I've got the bottles of pills ready and finished writing my will, I stop feeling anxious because I know that there is a way out. Before I discovered that, I thought that the anxiety that was tormenting me would never end.'

That is why observers who judge everything at face value are charmed by the reassuring sight of the lady who turns up at funerals, and by the serene calm of the man who has just made plans to commit suicide.

The image is a decoy that manipulates the emotions of those who are observing us. We watch the way others see us and, as we project a serene self-image, they react to it and we know that they are reacting. This interplay of deception and self-deception eventually creates a real relationship that can last a lifetime. But it exists on a knife edge.

This is why there are more victims' associations than survivors' associations. In the Middle Ages the victims were sentenced alongside their assailants because they were too close to them, but our modern cultural obligations mean that we have to run to help the victims. We now have a tendency to be suspicious of survivors. Who do they think they are? Do they think they're immortal? Do they think they are superhuman?

So the survivors begin to feel ashamed of their pride. 'When I saw that all my friends had been killed and that I was the only survivor, I experienced a great jubilation. I had escaped death. As soon as help came, I felt ashamed of feeling so happy and did all I could to help. They thought I was very brave.' A combination of survivor guilt and a feeling of power makes survivors secretive: 'If the others knew, they would think badly of me.'

When being ashamed of being happy
leads to misunderstandings, resilient children
run to help the weak

A child who grows up in a stable environment acquires the stable responses characteristic of that environment. But when an extreme encounter with death suddenly removes a child from his environment, his feelings are confused. It is as though he were saying, in the same sentence, 'I am guilty and I am innocent. I am one of the chosen and I am ashamed of being proud.' When a child is tortured by guilt, it is not easy for him to say, 'My parents were shot because I disobeyed them.' The survivor then becomes obsequious and only too ready to take orders. But he rebels every night and as he appears before the imaginary court he invents as he falls asleep, he protests as loudly as he can in an attempt to defend and justify himself. When he sees a weakling in the schoolyard next day, he runs to help him. If society provides institutional care for the weak, he will probably find ways to express the arguments he dreamed up the night before, but if he relies upon images, he will probably be misunderstood.

When Huong saw Thanh enter the home where he had been placed after being wounded, he was immediately drawn to the newcomer, who had a wooden leg. Huong would have preferred to have had a playmate who was livelier and more forward, but he could not abandon little Thanh to his loneliness without feeling embarrassed. So he played nicely with him. Delighted that someone had at last looked at him as though he were a normal child, Thanh began to play fight with him, and Huong did not dare refuse to join in. Thanh was so weak that Huong had no difficulty in gently bending him over backwards and tripping him up, but he also helped him by breaking his fall and lowering him to the ground.

At this point, the nurses rushed up, beat Huong in the name of morality and gave him a telling off. As the children gathered to go into the refectory, they humiliated him in front of everyone, telling the other children how far Huong was willing to take advantage of his strength to bully someone weaker than him.

Retreating into his inner world during this sermon, just as he had done throughout the war, Huong remained calm, even though he had been humiliated. He knew that he was one of the elite because he had triumphed over death more than once. He knew that he was a superhuman being who was better than these nurses, who were just mere mortals who understood nothing.

Survivors find the fantasy of appearing before an inner court comforting. They are attacked but in the end they are justified because the court allows them to plead a case that grants them the right to live: 'The nurses passed judgement on me. But I'm the superman. I'm the one who is right.' In extreme situations, the real quickly becomes a support for fantasies.

The courts they dream of allow survivors to be rehabilitated. As in the concentration camps described by Vasily Grossman in the early chapters of *Life and Fate*, they are not guilty.[24] They were compelled to act as they did by obscure forces and a heavy weight – millions of tonnes – is pressing down on them. No one who is alive can be innocent. They are all guilty: the defendant, the prosecutor and anyone who thinks about the defendant, the prosecutor or the judge. They do not know why it hurts so much, or why they are so ashamed of their abjectness.

'OK,' says the orphan, 'I'm alive because I killed him. And yet I'm innocent. It's the real world that's gone mad. If only you knew how it happened. You wouldn't believe me. I am one of the chosen because I'm the only one left. I'm still standing and the dead are lying all around me. I am small, desolate, guilty, despairing, chosen, grandiose, euphoric and ashamed. But don't pity me, whatever you do. I am stronger than death.'

A child who has survived an extreme situation is shaped like an oxymoron: his guilt is innocent, his pride is shameful and his heroism is cowardly; he was found guilty in his age of innocence; he is ashamed because he is proud of having survived when the people he loved did not make it, and his heroism proves to him that he was a coward because, if he had really been brave, he would have died along with his family.

The environment plays a major role in shaping this oxymoron. All victors are suspect, and all victims are lovable. It is not unusual for an institution that takes in a child to express its disgust when it learns that he or she is the victim of a rape. Readers often delight in leafing through books about the death camps. Adults sometimes enjoy the disgust they feel for the orphaned children they are looking after so kindly. When an adult acts out the scenario in which he is helping a poor child, he often says to himself that he is both generous and better than the child because he is acting out the part of the man who is kind to the unfortunate. The child therefore learns to be loved because he is unhappy. And woe betide him if he gets better; the adult would have no reason to go on loving him.

The admiration we feel for victorious children is also ambivalent. When a discourse becomes too logical, it ceases to be psychological. When an adult says, 'I admire this child. She's a little fighter,' he cannot admit to himself that he is thinking, 'I hate her for doing so well at school when my own daughter is failing ... And besides, what did she have to do in order to survive? Definitely killed someone, prostituted herself for sure. Otherwise she'd be dead, like the rest of them.'

The fate of Roseline provides a typical example of the ambivalence we feel towards resilient children. The first thing we say is, 'She was beautiful when she was deported at the age of seventeen.' Then we express surprise at how successful she has been in both social and intellectual terms. And then one day we add, 'It must have been terrible for her. It turns out that she survived because she prostituted herself.' That is the classic scenario. We love victims so long as they remain wretched because it makes us feel good when we help them. But when the martyrs turn into heroes and become powerful, they become suspect because it is unnatural for prey animals to turn into predators.

And besides, survivors are the bringers of bad news. They wear us out with their misfortunes. Talking about incest over dinner is in very poor taste. Are they talking about their ordeal to make us feel guilty? Or to make us cry? Or to demand a bigger pension?

And finally, survivors are immoral because life has been good to them, even though their families died. In a culture of melancholy, there is always something unclean about celebrations.[25] There is something shameful about being happy when our parents are dying. And that is what happens with resilient children who refuse to go under together with their loved ones.

The solidarity we admire blocks the resilience we admire; the death of a loved one can set our creativity free, but no one dares admit it

Mouloud was very good-looking and was doing so well in the sixth form that his teachers advised him to apply for university. That same evening, the doctor had to be called because Mouloud's stomach pains were so bad that he had lost consciousness. After regaining consciousness and thinking about it for a while, Mouloud realized that he was suffering extreme anxiety at the idea of abandoning his mother and his nine younger brothers and sisters. Studying hard and the possibility of success meant leaving his mother on her own. She was a widow and she was illiterate. She would never be able to bring up the children on her own. The anxiety disappeared after a few days. Mouloud had found a way out: he would make sure that he failed his exams. The immediate relief cost him personal fulfilment and the social success he could have hoped for. Everyone greatly admired Mouloud for his altruism and for making such a sacrifice. Funeral orations were made for his academic success. But no one dared to see that, if Mouloud was to blossom, his mother would die and his brothers and sisters would be taken into institutional care. That was the price that would have had to be paid before Mouloud could become resilient.

Proust, Freud and Max Weber are perfect examples of the 'take-off of creativity' after the death of their fathers.[26] The process of mourning allows the young adult to attain the mental autonomy he dared not adopt while his father was still alive.

Joyce and Pascal experienced the same liberation through mourning. I have personally observed the post-mourning 'take-off of creativity' on several occasions. When he was seventeen, Robert was terribly inhibited. He did not dare to speak to his parents or look them in the eye, or go out with his friends, to say nothing of flirting with girls. 'The day I realized that my mother was going to die because the bullet to her head had done too much damage, my anxiety vanished. I felt astonishingly free and light. I cried a lot when she died because I loved her dearly. But I felt free because I no longer had to make her wishes come true. I could go my own way without hurting her.' Over the next ten years Robert did brilliantly in his law exams, travelled the world as a freelance journalist working for a major newspaper, bought a magnificent house and fathered four children.

Patricia admired her father, who was a major political figure. When he died following a sudden heart attack, she was in despair. But she was amazed at how light she felt afterwards. She stopped having attacks of anxiety. She took over the running of the house. She started going to her dance classes again and was bold enough to find a new job; it was her father who had found her old job for her, and it was driving her to distraction. Her old job meant that she was doing what her father wanted her to do; now that he was dead, she could take a job that suited her better.

Show the survivors no mercy. They are killers, not victims. To make them pay the price for the crime of surviving, we have to ask them to create something.

There are many more orphans in creative circles than in the elite schools or in the population at large.[27] Seventeen of the thirty-five writers mentioned in school textbooks on French literature suffered the early loss of one or both parents. And the list of young orphans who became famous writers gets longer and longer: 'Baudelaire, the Brontë sisters, Byron, Coleridge, Dante, Dostoyevsky, Dumas, Poe, Rousseau, Sand, Swift, Tolstoy, Voltaire . . . and I could cite many other studies that would make the list still longer.'[28]

The picture is not, however, completely rosy: longitudinal studies of orphan groups show that many of them do better than the children of parents who divorce and that they tend to work in the cultural sector, but the same studies also show that the same groups will include a fair number of delinquents.[29]

We are now in a position to explain why the absence of structure is so often associated with both creativity and delinquency. The overbearing structure of a close family or a society that is too well organized makes a child feel safe. But, because it forces children to develop along lines laid down by their parents or by society, it blocks their creativity, as the only thing they learn is how to do what they are told to do. Orphans who have been set free from these constraints by some family tragedy may encounter a host structure that is prepared to listen to them. If they do, they find themselves in a marginal position that encourages them to talk about their ordeal and to discover new ways of seeing the world. They are in a position to become creative and to join the ranks of the many scientific innovators and artists who are, by definition, marginal because they are introducing into our culture something that was not there before they emerged.

Studies of migrants also tell us that, when young people do not have the support of some emotional or social structure, the intensity of their desires cannot be channelled. And when large quantities of energy are not put to good use, they are transformed into a violence that can explode at any moment. Like migrants, orphans whose family or social structures have been destroyed can become creators if they are given room to express themselves, but they can just as easily become delinquents if their energy finds no outlet.

These brief comments on orphans, migrants, delinquents and innovators suggest that their organic talent for survival is influenced by their environment, whereas the ways in which they survive within that environment are influenced by collective acts.[30]

The numbness induced by a terrible trauma often leaves fewer traces than an insidious wound; the impassionate damage inflicted by a myth can do more harm than passionate hatred

During the war in Mozambique, tens of thousands of children aged between six and twelve witnessed massacres, underwent torture and were sometimes involved in both. In many cases, a child with a gun kept watch while his friends decapitated his parents, dismembered their bodies and impaled their heads.[31] For most of the time, those children were stupefied. A witness who trusted in first impressions would say that what had happened meant nothing to them. They were in fact numb, physically inert and mentally numb. Their need to be in denial was so vital that they had to understand nothing, on pain of death.

When one subsequently sees them smile, one wonders how they contrived not to die on the spot. Had they been alone, they would certainly have died, as we sometimes see with children who switch between apparent stupefaction and uncontrollable outbursts of rage against everything and against themselves. But these children adapt because they are in denial, and survive because they are not alone. It is the qualities of the bonds that they were able to weave before or immediately after the trauma that determines the quality of their resilience.

The children who had been made vulnerable before their ordeal because they had been abandoned or because their families were ill did not survive. In many cases, they lost their minds and became catatonic, absent, confused or dreamy. In contrast, those who had been stabilized by a permanent bond succeeded in finding a few defence mechanisms, such as denial or hatred.

Those who had the support of a stable structure, a few social rituals or a role to play or something to do at the time of the tragedy were more likely to survive than those who just happened to be there and witnessed it by accident.

They will come back to life after the tragedy if they are integrated into a group or if they have to take on some responsibility. The enormous wound that is embedded in them will, however, gradually find ways of expressing itself as they grow up. They appear to be intact, but their life trajectories have, insidiously, been completely thrown off course.

Even when we are talking about psychology we think like car mechanics, rather as though a single cause could have an overall effect: as if a huge childhood trauma explains all subsequent suffering in the same way that a blocked carburettor explains an engine splutter. When it is 'obvious' to us what has happened, it can blind us in the same way that light can dazzle us. Indeed, in some cases an acute and spectacular trauma does less damage than a chronic and insidious one.

Acute traumas are obviously damaging, but are their effects longer lasting than those of incessant constraints that leave their mark on the memory and modify the emotions, the learning process and the feeling of self-hood? Victims who are stunned by intense violence often react by losing consciousness. When they do remain conscious, their anxiety is so great that they experience the extraordinary feeling of witnessing their own tragedy. Dostoyevsky saw himself sitting on his bed, and Nietzsche imagined that he was following his own funeral procession. But when the emotion is so intense as to trigger a state of mental confusion that brings back images from the dream or the momentary delirium, the incidental mental confusion leaves few traces in the memory.

When, on the other hand, these wounded souls live in a petrified culture that judges them at a glance and then never revises its opinion, they become victims for a second time. In this case, it is the family, institutional or social environment that saved them which prevents them from recovering. During the Second World War children in care were saved by their foster families. Without them, they would have died. In those days children without families almost inevitably ended up as farm boys or skivvies. So, after having taken them in, their new employers beat them as soon as they were within reach, or humiliated them in ways that meant nothing to them. Seven-year-old Bernard spent six months living in a barn. He slept on a bale of straw, never washed and never even scraped the mud off his clothes because he worked so hard, starting at five in the morning. His repulsive appearance confirmed the public stereotype of children in care. The boy himself took the view that his fate was enviable because he regularly succeeded in dodging the farmer's blows and was invited to eat with the farmhands on Sundays, when they amused themselves by getting him drunk. In the child's inner world, the fact that he could dodge the blows proved how agile he was, whilst getting drunk on Sunday allowed him to integrate himself into the adult world.

Brigitte, a twelve-year-old hunchback, was a skivvy on the same farm. Because she was a girl, she had a proper bed, and even sheets. Her domestic tasks included taking off the farmhands' muddy boots when they came into the house. She would crouch down in front of them and pull off the clogs whilst the men pushed their other foot against the girl's chest 'to help her'. When the clog came off, the child would fall backwards, head over heels, and everyone would laugh. Bernard thought that the little girl's fate was no more enviable than his, even though she had sheets on her bed.

During a trauma, the dissolution of consciousness, or even the denial that blocks out the unbearable part of reality, protects the victim in the same way that the amputation of a gangrenous limb protects an injured person from septicaemia. But when the psychotrauma becomes chronic, insidious and is repeated day after day, the disorders it imprints on the child are less visible but longer lasting, and they permeate her personality throughout her development. To make matters worse, Brigitte could not say anything about what had happened. Every night, she relived a stylized version of those humiliating scenes as she lay in bed. Bernard, on the other hand, used the Sunday drinking bouts as an excuse to act the hero. In the barn he would boast to the other kids about how he had played the clown and about the imaginary fights he had won.

In cases of severe trauma, what is being imprinted in the child's mind is, of course, the real, but it is above all a feeling of selfhood, as seen by the other. As she lay in her clean sheets at night, Brigitte constructed for herself the identity of a girl who had been humiliated, whereas Bernard, as he lay, covered in mud, on his bale of hay became the boy who had been drinking with the adults, and the boy who made them laugh.

This feeling of selfhood becomes a kind of embryonic identity, rather like an image of the self that has been implanted in the child by the gaze of the other: 'I am the one other people look at with horrified disgust because they know that I was born as the result of a rape . . . In their eyes, I'm carrying the plague.' So long as the memory persists, it will have the power to shape the child's personality: its long-term effects persist because memory works in the long term, but as the child's personality becomes more structured, the gaze of the other tends to trigger only short-lived emotions. A child who is hyper-attentive to others and whose memories are fresh will think for a long time that 'I am so disgusting, so defiled. I'm a monster because that is how grown-ups see me. So it is only natural that they should steer me towards those social areas that are reserved for the disgusting, the defiled and the monsters of this world.' An adult who is viewed with disgust, but whose sense of self was originally shaped by an affectionate gaze, will, in contrast, tend to think: 'What's wrong with him? Why's he looking at me like that? Who does he think he is?' And that feeling of irritation, which was implanted in him by the gaze of others, tends, rather, to find expression in anger or avoidance, and will have no lasting effects.

The cold violence that insidiously shapes a feeling of selfhood is constantly reproduced by tiny behaviours, by the minor actions and banal words that structure the environment in which the child has to grow up. When a boy in care says 'I want to pass my exams and become a lawyer,' we do not have to say much to shatter his dreams. A raised eyebrow, a pout of disgust or a gaze that lingers for a few seconds is all it takes to tell him: 'I've said something stupid. That's an impossible dream for a kid in care.' When addressed to a lawyer who grew up in care, the same behavioural scenario will trigger a completely different emotion because the adult's history allows him to give it a different meaning, rather as though he were thinking to himself: 'You think it's impossible. My social achievements prove that you are wrong and that you don't understand anything.' For a child who still does not know who he is, or what his worth is, the gaze has the power to discourage him completely. But for an adult who already has a history, the same behaviour triggers a momentary feeling of cheerful condescension: 'He doesn't understand anything: my life proves him wrong.'

This chronic violence and the behavioural indices that never make the news and cannot be integrated into a story probably have a devastating effect on personalities that are still developing, and their effects may be more long term than acute traumas, which are easier to talk about. The inner worlds of the young Palestinians who now survive in the Gaza Strip and their Israeli counterparts in Hebron have been shaped by insidious violence. However, its effects are greater but less conscious than those of terrible tragedies that are easier to mythologize.[32]

The massacre of the Palestinians as they prayed at the Tomb of the Patriarchs was immediately integrated into every clan's mythology in order to trigger the indignation and anger that fuel courage. But it is, perhaps, the minor day-to-day but repeated incidents that inculcate hatred into every Palestinian child. Once the sense of self has been imbued with hatred, it leaves unconscious traces in the memory.

The nationalist propaganda of the 1930s taught French schoolchildren to hate the Boche. A chance meeting with a German, an outburst of raucous laughter or a guttural *Heraus* was therefore all it took to justify the horror that had been implanted in the memories of those French children. In such cases, reality supplies the children's feelings with alibis for the coldness of their institutional violence. Now that German and French children have been shaped by a different daily context, they can tidy up their grandfathers' graves together. Yet the myth still teaches us that the Germans laid Europe to waste, whereas their deadly ideology in fact did as much to destroy Germany as the rest of Europe.

It is easier to turn an acute trauma into a play or story. We can easily turn it into images, stories or wonderful tragic epics that celebrate the exploits of heroes. But how can we construct a myth with a shrug of the shoulders that destroys hope, or with a scornful smile that shatters a dream? A tragic event can be made to undergo a metamorphosis, but how can we represent a gesture of which we have no awareness?

If we wish to transform horror, we must create places where emotions can be expressed; resocializing children 'as though nothing had happened' emphasizes their wounds, but they can easily be transformed if we can draw them, put them on stage, or turn them into a story or a political demand

As soon as the Croatian children fleeing the fighting in Vukovar entered the refugee camp in Spansko, they began to draw pictures of the ordeals they had just lived through.³³ For children, drawing pictures is a way of talking. Their pictures taught these children to speak and their drawings allowed them to tell the history of the war.

At first, the 210 refugee children, who were aged between three and seven, were resocialized in local schools. But what they had just been through imbued them with the exceptional feeling that they did not belong to the world of normal children who attended school and had parents.

Because they had been resocialized too quickly, they had an exaggerated sense of their own abnormality. So they cried, screamed and hit out. The process of resocialization is difficult because asking traumatized children who have witnessed horrors to mix with children who have been well socialized heightens their feeling of being 'not like the others'. Conversely, keeping the 'abnormal' children together does nothing to improve their self-image, especially as the gaze of other children labels them as poor and rather repulsive victims.

The most effective way to resocialize them is to transform the trauma (and this can, as it happens, be done quite quickly). As soon as we can talk about a trauma, draw it, put it on a stage or think it through, we can control the emotions that either overwhelmed us or made us freeze when it occurred. Representing the tragedy allows us to rework the feelings it triggers.

Children who have survived horrific experiences are still imbued with a feeling of horror but have yet to learn the rituals of their own culture. Many of the young Cambodians who went back to school after spending several years in the camps did not know that they should not get out their textbooks when they were sitting exams. Their teachers accused them of cheating. As a result of this misunderstanding, their relationship with their teachers was as troubled as their emotions.

After the Second World War Renate Sprengel had to deal with a group of Italian children aged between eight and eleven who had lost both their parents.[34] For the last few years they had, like so many *sciucia*, survived on the streets by shining shoes, begging and stealing a little food. They slept wherever they could, and were often beaten up and raped. When Renate took them in she was surprised to see that they behaved in two very different but related ways: the children were numb with shock but they also got into lots of fights.

Forty years later, exactly the same pattern of behaviour was observed in the Vukovar children. 'They seem to me to be too well-behaved, and you do not hear the usual background noise typical of children of their age.'[35] They kept to themselves, did not play much, sucked their thumbs, fiddled with their hair, and never swung their arms as they walked around. They stared straight ahead of them and never blinked.

This ethological description provides a clue as to what their inner world was like: they had been in denial for so long that they felt empty inside. This meant that, whilst they felt no pain, they could not create a mental life for themselves. The stereotypical way in which they moved did, however, allow them to create a sort of ersatz life. For them, creating a mental void within themselves was a defence mechanism. Whenever anyone tried to help them, they were overwhelmed by their own emotions. They could not stand this, and so they transformed their emotions into violence. When Giorgio, who had spent three years living on the streets of Rome, was placed in an institution, a well-meaning counsellor gave him a toy that had belonged to her own son: a little zinc aeroplane. Out of his mind with joy, Giorgio was overwhelmed by the affection he felt for her, but the affection immediately turned into anxiety. He flung the plane down and kicked it against the wall until it was broken. Happiness is very close to anxiety when there is no ritual to teach the child how to control it. This is what we see with babies who begin to cry when the laughter goes on too long.

Children are saturated by their environment. When that environment is full of horrors, they become empty inside so as to feel no pain, in the same way that adults lose consciousness or shield their faces to avoid seeing a terrifying reality. But when their emotions are reawakened, these children have not learned to control them. The emotion triggered by a happy event is all the more intense because their inner emptiness allowed them to avoid uncontrollable emotions. So they give hugs or lash out, and it is all the same to them. What becomes of that emotional reaction depends, however, upon how the adult interprets it. If the adult sees a child like this as a worthless monster, he or she will design a curriculum for worthless monsters. The child adapts to it by learning how to get into fights. But if the teacher understands that children like this have not had the opportunity to learn to control their emotions, she will provide them with places where they can come to terms with the horrors they have experienced.

All these children suffer from anxiety and emotional problems that have physical repercussions. Alopecia, sleep disorder and eating disorders are all common. And yet, within only a few years, half of them will have no obvious problems. They will be hitting their targets at school and will be learning as they should. Indeed, 'most of them will display ... an age-appropriate aptitude for learning, and may overcompensate by making a very positive investment in pre-school tasks'.[36] For these children, school often becomes a place of happiness. They make friends with other boys and girls there. They play a lot. For the first time in their lives, the adults they meet are not killers. They learn that adults can actually be kind, and their regular presence teaches them the rituals that structure emotions. Their experience of being loved and being in a happy place for the first time explains why it is not unusual to see these children getting to school before it opens, and shivering with cold outside the gates.

Their fate depends on how the social gaze sees them. If their problems are seen as proof that they are of poor quality, they will be steered towards institutions for poor-quality children and will learn to become delinquents. Others will be steered towards an acculturated environment, and will see school as a happy place where they can transform the horrors they have seen. Anna Freud eventually came to take the view that vulnerability cannot be explained in terms of the child's individual characteristics, and had to be understood in more general terms.[37] The way the child progresses along its developmental lines and matures depends upon the interaction between many favourable external influences, and the evolution of internal structures.

A gardener who can cast spells, a big sister/mentor or a political party can change the meaning of suffering

Marie-Rose Moro identifies one specific factor in these 'developmental lines' or 'guiding stars': 'Somewhere in the social environment of those migrants' children who do well at school, there is a figure who plays the "mentor" role. In the case of Abdolaye, for example, it was a teacher; in the case of Hamina, it was a big sister, and in that of Hamid it was the kindly woman who lived next door.'[38]

Because it is over-functional, our culture under-estimates the role of mentors. Deprived children are so eager to identify that it does not take much to give them a 'developmental line'. But all too often, our cultures are trapped in their public discourses and do not provide them with even a single guiding star.

Maurice spent the first ten years of his life in the company of his alcoholic parents, who fought every day. At the age of ten he was placed in institutional care. He was not unhappy. But one day he met a gardener who brought some magic into his life. Every day, the boy would wait for the gardener, eager to ask him a few banal questions. The man answered them patiently. For the adult, taking a few moments off work to answer a boy's questions meant nothing. For the little boy, it was a big event and it was fabulous because it was the first time in his life that someone had said a kind word to him and given him the opportunity to listen to stories about flowers. Maurice is now an academic, and it was he who told me the fable of the gardener, of the mentor who, with a single word or a single gesture, eased his pain.

A child who is exposed to a life-threatening risk or sudden acculturation is forced to change and has to undergo a metamorphosis.[39] 'If the child can stand up to this transcultural threat, and can find in his own capacities or his environment facts that allow him to neutralize the threat, he becomes convinced that he is out of the ordinary and almost invulnerable, until some event reactivates the buried memory of the danger he was in.'[40]

Resilience has nothing to do with invulnerability. A child may feel invulnerable because he is out of the ordinary, but that does not mean that he is. Besides, life often reminds him that he is not when a very minor event touches the painful part of his memory and reawakens it.

Child soldiers look invulnerable: they are cute, stand guard very bravely, ask you very nicely for your papers in their high-pitched voices, and will shoot to kill if you make just one wrong move. And then they go home after their day's work is done. They have killed in the way that good children kill because weapons technology enables them to do so and because the adults around them have turned murder into a rite of passage.

Everything is fine so long as these children are not socialized because, for them, murder means social advancement. But when they go back to school after the war and when the context changes, their personalities begin to develop once more. It is now that the post-traumatic syndrome appears. It is only when their empathy is sufficiently developed for them to put themselves in someone else's position and to imagine how they suffered that their actions acquire the meaning of murder. It is only then that they begin to suffer themselves. The appearance of anxiety and guilt proves that they are on the road to becoming human beings. A child who kills and goes on smiling remains invulnerable so long as he cannot empathize with others. His strength demonstrates his limitations. A resilient child will have transformed his pain. The child soldier may become resilient when he tries to understand how he could do what he did.

It is, therefore, the context created by adults that gives events their meaning. Killing a man can mean victory or murder, and its meaning can either make us feel exhilarated or torment us.

When we are old enough to look back at our lives, the way we see our past can change the meaning of what happened to us and of the feeling of imminent death. Jeannette and Joseph were on the same transport from Drancy to Auschwitz. But Joseph succeeded in escaping before the doors of the trucks were sealed. Jeannette survived because the train she was on reached the camp just before it was liberated. When he got back to Paris, Joseph waited for her in the plush surroundings of the Hôtel Lutétia. He felt a terrible pain in his stomach when he saw the number tattooed in blue on his sister's forearm.[41] At a time when that tattoo was a mark of shame, Jeannette never wore anything but long-sleeved blouses. In the post-war years, both Joseph and Jeannette were active in the Communist Party, which sang their praises and told them that they were going to bring happiness and justice into the world. As time passed, and thanks to the speeches, the celebrations and the egalitarian parades, Jeannette gradually began to wear blouses with shorter sleeves. Thirty years later, by which time society had discovered the horrors of the camps and had learned how to talk about them in public, Jeannette was wearing only short-sleeved blouses. In this new context, the tattoo meant 'I came back from the camps and I can bear witness. I have the right to speak.'

The longer a survivor lives, the further away death seems to be. When Jeannette was billeted in the Hôtel Lutétia, her tattoo meant: 'I almost died a terrible death.' Fifty years later, the blue number tattooed on her skin meant that she had played a clever trick. 'I conned them out of fifty years of my life. I really tricked them! I really should have died. Every day I survive, I give death the V sign!'

'The older I got, the more death retreated!' said Jorge Semprun.[42] For damaged children the feeling of living on borrowed time can be very intense. Every night Alain, who had leukaemia as a child, used to pray: 'Please God, let me live until I am ten.' Now that he has been cured, every passing year takes him further away from death. So it is possible: we can transform our pain.

It is difficult to observe a river when you are swimming in it; so long as violence was seen as a normal educational method, the idea of abuse was inconceivable

When disaster strikes from afar, and when the violence is caused by a foreign army, a gang of armed men or a natural disaster, it is the historical context that gives the event meaning and that allows us to face up to and change our ordeal. When the aggression comes from people we love, the work of transformation is much more difficult.

The notion of 'the abused child' has a curious history. For a long time the idea of abuse was inconceivable. When one in two children died in the first year of life, when one could 'lose two or three without too much grief' (Montaigne) and when a child could be regarded as a 'hubbub of meaning' (Bossuet), to hit, beat or imprison one would never be interpreted as abuse by an adult man.

Infanticide was for a long time seen as a form of social

hygiene. As Seneca put it: 'What is good must be set apart from what is good for nothing.'[43] The father therefore decided the fate of children of dubious parentage, of the malformed, of a girl or boy he did not want: 'A citizen of Rome did not "have" a child; he "took" a child and "raised him up" (*tollere*).'[44] Paulus, who was a jurist during the reign of the Emperor Severus, even described ways of getting rid of children of dubious parentage: throw them out into the street, smother them or let them starve. Education was based on terror: the whip, brutality – both in private and in public – and excessive punishments. To cite Seneca once more: 'Parents subject the still malleable characters of their children to what will do them good ... Let them cry and struggle as they will ... we will instil liberal culture into them by means of terror if they refuse to learn.'[45]

The history of the Middle Ages is full of stories of children being drowned, smothered, abandoned, sold to rich neighbours or to the Saracens, who made slaves of them.

The nineteenth century did away with slavery but invented industry. Children were sent to work in factories, where their low wages and their docility meant that they could be forced to work fifteen hours a day, huddled into recesses, harnessed to tubs of coal or crawling through mine tunnels. The children went bald, in the same way that the overworked children in modern-day India become blond when they are suffering from iron deficiency, or that the faces of undernourished girls become covered in black hair, or that the hair of boys under stress can turn white overnight.

The terrifying conditions in which these children lived were never described as 'abuse' because they were normal. Beating them, mutilating them, isolating them, starving, humiliating, raping and abandoning them so as to avoid having to drown them, seemed normal to adults who were imbued with the beliefs of their time. The miraculous thing is that, despite the tortures they endured as children, some of them did grow up to become adults who did not reproduce the brutality of their culture. They are a good example of resilience in children.

The notion of abuse became widespread only in the 1970s. It was probably thanks to the efforts of a few resilient adults who had been abused as children that it began to be talked about. The idea of resilience was beginning to emerge, but resilience itself has been part of the real world for as long as human beings have been human beings.

It was definitely a shift in public discourse that changed children's fate. When we look at the real age, at the time of death, of the skeletons found in grave sites from the Neolithic period to modern times, we are horrified to see how many of the bones are those of children. From the end of the nineteenth century onwards, child mortality rates began to fall. This was probably due not to improved hygiene or nutrition – both remained abysmal – but to a cultural shift in the way babies were regarded. So long as it could be said that the murder of a one-year-old was nothing more than a late abortion, the death rate remained alarmingly high. So long as it could be thought that children who had not reached the age of reason were no more than perverse animals, the number of fatal 'accidents' remained very high. But once it was realized that babies are small human beings who are still developing and that they are intelligent enough to understand much of our adult world at a very early age, it was found that very simple measures are all it takes to protect them.

Until the mid-nineteenth century, death controlled the environment in which children had to grow up. Very few children were brought up by their parents because many women died very young (often in their twenties) and few men lived beyond the age of forty.[46] Consequently, about one child in two was raised by adults who were not their natural parents. There was no need for divorce, because the number of early deaths meant that remarriages were common. In the event of marital conflict, all the offended party had to do was wait.

Technological innovation has a major influence on how conjugality is structured; and social discourses establish the rules that define how children develop

Technological innovation has always had a great influence on the way forms of conjugality are structured.[47] When the iron ploughshare was invented in the eleventh century, the weight of a man was enough to make it slice through the soil. Harvests became abundant enough to make famine a thing of the past. Women were to stay at home and bring six or seven children into the world. At the time, this was seen as a major step forward that improved the position of women. Children now began to live in a completely different environment. From the twelfth century onwards groups of women, rather like the polymaternal families that can still be seen in Africa or Martinique, brought up their children together. The children's development was perfectly normal. Just who their fathers were was uncertain because they were rarely at home and because monogamous marriage was not the rule. It was only following the Council of Trent (1545–63) that the Church began to advocate marriage and the asceticism that went with it, and that Church and King began to ask women to 'denounce the fathers'.[48] This moral shift reveals how technology and the state play a major role in shaping the idea of paternity. It was only from the nineteenth century onwards that fathers were integrated into the educational cell and became the state's representatives within the family.[49] Marriage finally came to be strictly defined when the factories and the bourgeoisie needed couples to structure industrial society.

Children have therefore grown up in many different family environments according to the technology and philosophy of different periods. As the clan gave way to the family unit, as abandonment was replaced by overprotection, as permissiveness gave way to constraint, and as torture gave way to adoration, so adults were produced who were able to transmit both life and a culture.

Whilst there are no lessons to be learned from history, the comparative method does allow us to shed some light on our own problems. What does the current overinvestment in children in the West mean? It probably means that we have arrived at a better understanding of early childhood thanks to the advances that have been made by the observational sciences, and thanks to a discourse that regards individual fulfilment as a cultural value. The printed word has facilitated the development of the schools that give the qualifications that structure new social classes and their inequalities. Dazzling technological innovations mean that we now inhabit an artificial environment in which muscular energy and the strength that comes from violence are

largely redundant. More important still, medical repro-
ductive technologies have completely changed the
meaning of life. Girls are no longer our servants, and
boys are no longer walking sticks for our old age. Our
children's mission is to make our dreams come true, to
become individuals and then to leave us.

Migratory movements are in effect carrying out
natural experiments that allow us to observe how
couples are structured and why they take determinate
forms. Over the last thirty years or so, the Ivory Coast
has been turned upside down by economic constraints
and technological developments that have driven people
into the cities. In 1964 a new law on marriage changed
conjugality completely.[50] Until then, the function of
arranged marriage had been to perpetuate group structures and to pass on their technologies and traditions.
Emotional commitment was of secondary importance,
and relations between the partners who married were
often lukewarm. After 1964 love replaced social constraint as the rationale for marriage. The children of
those new-style couples are now almost twenty years
old. They grew up with parents who were close to
one another, and with structures that placed the
emphasis on individual happiness rather than respect
for tradition.

The grandmothers remained in the countryside.
Cut off in the cities, young mothers forgot the rituals
that prescribed how they should behave towards

their babies within the space of a single generation. The force that once shaped their children now stemmed from the mother's personality and not the tradition of the group. The emotional world in which their children were immersed and which helped to shape their emotional lives was no longer the same. When young people live together because they are in love, the emphasis falls on individuals and not the group. So much so that, when a couple begins to have personal differences, the emphasis is still on individual fulfilment, and they begin to talk of divorce. The earliest experience of children who have grown up in such a conjugal climate was the warmth of the emotional prison created by parents who are in love but who know little about tradition. Social roles were less clearly defined, and the cultural role of their fathers was unclear. When they were about ten, many of these children experienced an emotional chill when their parents split up.

The role of their absentee fathers became even more blurred. Their wretched mothers were overworked. And the traditional family, which had never really been part of their day-to-day life or of the stories they were told, was unable to take over or offer an alternative. The technological and legal changes that took place in the culture of their parents explain why so many children of that generation, who grew up in a gentle, loving prison, suddenly found themselves living in an emotional wilderness in which they had no cultural markers to guide them on their way.

Although their personalities have clearly improved, there has been a significant rise in the incidence of depression and the number of suicides, which are almost twice as common in single-parent and reconstructed families.[11] The explanation for these ordeals does not lie in poverty, as they can be observed at all levels of society. Their roots lie, rather, in a lack of emotional bodybuilding: these children have made the transition from a family cocoon to social aggression with no cultural signposts to guide them on their way.

In the West, the era in which having a large family was a demonstration of parental morality is coming to a close. Our individualist culture no longer makes a virtue of having a large family, because large families mean that parents have to devote their efforts to supporting their children. The criterion for morality in the West is now respect for the individual who, if he or she is to flourish, must limit the number of children he or she has and, if need be, contemplate divorce. These are completely different lifestyles and reconciling the two would be very difficult.

These brief remarks allow us to understand that the meaning of 'children' is constantly changing and that the environment we force upon our children depends on our idea of what children are. As technology grows richer, modes of individual development change, and laws tend to follow social trends by approving or forbidding certain lines of development. In cultures where it is natural for children to die and where violence is an adaptive value, infanticide and rape are not criminalized.[52] There can be no concept of abuse in such a context. Children are destined to die and suffer, or must become resilient if they wish to survive.

In a culture in which there are few children and in which individuality is a value, abuse becomes something that cannot be tolerated, and this encourages three lines of research: detecting and describing abuse; understanding its effects by observing how abused children grow up; and trying to find ways to care for them.

Tracing the history of the idea of abuse is a curious exercise: it reveals the real existence of a phenomenon of which we were unaware because it did not stand out but merged into the ambient culture. When abandoning children was commonplace, it was impossible to see abuse as a crime because 'everyone' abandoned children until 1924. Adults who beat children, got them drunk, worked them to death and sexually abused them were not punished because it was, until 1941, acceptable behaviour. In its fight against poverty, which is a serious form of social abuse, industrial Britain built generous institutions and put children in workhouses. Abuse within the workhouse was inconceivable: a workhouse was a charitable institution. Only a few marginal and ungrateful individuals like Charles Dickens dared to say that children suffered in the workhouse.

After its victory of 1870 Prussia turned harshness into an educational principle. In Prussia's boarding schools the suffering was constant. It was only in recent decades that England's schools stopped inflicting painful and humiliating corporal punishments. And our devoted church schools once had no qualms about putting the young children entrusted to them in solitary confinement for days at a time. The most serious form of mental abuse possible was, in other words, inflicted on them in the name of morality.

The children suffered, and learned to hate the army, religion and school.[53] And yet many of them did survive, and even thanked their cruel teachers for having equipped them for life.

A new concept: abuse

It was in 1889 that some people in France began to think that it was wrong to abuse children and passed the first laws punishing abusive parents.[54]

But it was not until the 1950s that a neuro-surgeon named Ingraham, a paediatrician named Caffey and a radiologist named Silverman described some mysterious bone lesions that could be attributed to repeated blows.[55] The fact that doctors were the first to shed light on the idea of abuse suggests that 'normal people' require proof before they can understand something that has no name. With their images and reports, doctors supplied the proof that made it possible to think about abuse. In contrast, the Armenians who fled Turkey and the children who came back from Auschwitz had no proof of what they had seen. Nor do today's Rwandan children, who have no photographs of massacres, no administrative orders and no death certificates to prove that whole communities have disappeared.

Things began to change in 1962, when the paediatrician C. H. Kempe published 'The Battered Child Syndrome'.[56] The paediatrician Pierre Strauss and Judge Jean-Pierre Rosenczveig subsequently sat on the commission established by European commissioner Jacques Barrot to investigate child abuse in France. The outcome was the law of 10 July 1989 which had the support of Hélène Dorlhac, secretary of state for the family. There are now many associations in France (AFIREM, Enfance et Partage, Fondation pour l'enfance, Ligue française pour la santé mentale and others). With the support of a few intellectual stars such as Pierre Manciaux and Michel Lemay, they have refined the notion of abuse and are looking at how to repair the damage that has been done by helping children to become resilient.

This illustrates an interesting problem: it is difficult

to think the unthinkable. The first reports are almost always greeted with indignation. The facile assumption is that the aggressor is a stranger who is evil, monstrous and easily identifiable. Woe betide anyone who challenges that assumption by pointing out that 97.5 per cent of murders and acts of violence occur inside the family,[57] that major criminals can be good looking and that incestuous fathers can be very charming.

Once the initial hypothesis has been posited by a few pioneers, who usually attract fierce criticism, it becomes a facile assumption and a cultural cliché. And then, everyone begins to see abusive parents and incestuous fathers everywhere.

A newspaper publishes flawed statistics showing that 400,000 children have been abused; wives accuse their husbands of sexually molesting their daughters to get a quick divorce; girls barricade themselves into their bedrooms because they are afraid of their fathers.[58]

As long as an exceptional situation is beyond our social understanding, denial can flourish. It is, however, difficult to adjust to exceptional events, either because we do not believe they happened because they are so exceptional or because we are too ready to believe they happened because they are so exceptional. That is why publishing statistics or league tables of abuse is a pointless exercise. The very notion of abuse depends upon the cultural context that either obscures it or sheds light on it. As for the victim, she can either get angry about it or see the abuse as a source of pride, depending on whether her culture uses such tragedies to make people laugh or to manipulate them. It is more helpful to try to describe what goes on in the inner world of the abused child and how abused children develop.

The less we know, the stronger our convictions are. Challenging a body of knowledge can result in an enjoyable debate, but challenging someone's convictions is tantamount to calling them a liar, a madman or an idiot. We are much more likely to get angry when we are defending an opinion than when we are developing an idea. The function of collective thought is religious rather than intellectual: when we all say the same thing together, we can love one another because we all have the same worldview. That is why our stereotypes mean so much to us. So we all say, 'These abused children are tormented souls . . . the prisons are full of them . . . they are emotionally dead . . . impulsive. In the nineteenth century, bastards were possessed by the devil; in the twentieth century, we spoke of "depraved children"; in François Truffaut's day, the same children were "maladjusted"; and now we say that they will repeat the abuse, that they will becomes abusers because they have been abused.'[59]

How not to monitor resilient children

The most reliable and laborious method of study consists in observing a cohort of abused children and trying to monitor them regularly for as long as possible. The method is described as 'the longitudinal catamnestic method: it allows us to examine the behaviours of a group of subjects who are known to have been subjected to the same type of assault and to verify the appearance of the effects that can result from such attacks'.[60]

When we study this subject, we are regularly surprised by the dissociation between what becomes of the victims twenty to thirty years later, and the accounts given by the care workers who had to treat them. All the professionals say: 'Abuse is passed on from generation to generation . . . the abused child grows up to become an abusive adult . . . That girl in the institution . . . I dealt with her mother and one day I'll be dealing with her daughter.' I've said it myself. All these comments are true, but they reflect a startling failure to collect certain data. I propose to call this 'professional bias'. Professionals only get to deal with the problem cases, or with victims who repeat the abuse and thus confirm the theory. The others, or those who survive, go their own sweet way and never come into contact with the professionals.

We therefore have to do some fieldwork, get out of

the laboratories and the institutions, and talk to some abused children who do not confirm the theory.

To say that abused children can grow up to become perfectly rounded adults is certainly not the same thing as saying that we have to abuse children in order to turn them into perfectly rounded adults. Even Serge Moscovici, whose childhood was blighted by the 'rock of totalitarianism' in Romania, could write: 'The fact that I escaped them or gave them the slip still surprises me . . . I feel sorry for those who had a happy childhood because they had nothing to overcome.'[61]

The tragic cases revealed by our culture feed into our social discourse. Many stories of resilience have never been told and have not been analysed.

The first study, dating from 1946, that really pioneered research into emotional deprivation is a perfect illustration of this professional bias.[62] This magnificent piece of work clearly and elegantly demonstrates the degree to which maternal deprivation during the 'critical period' of the first months of life regularly leads to an observable behavioural sequence.[63] In the first month, the children become weepy and cling to the observer. From the second month onwards, they refuse contact, lie prone in their cots most of the time, lose weight and become sleepless. In the third month they become inexpressive, vacant and almost lethargic. They then lie flat on their stomachs and let themselves die, even if they are given food. Those who do survive are severely retarded and become either mentally handicapped or delinquent.

This description, which is regularly confirmed by those who have occasion to deal with abandoned children, calls for a brief commentary. Spitz's work has become such an integral part of our culture that it is now difficult to visit a prison without being told that it is maternal deprivation that causes delinquency.

As early as 1946 Spitz himself was talking about possible recuperation: 'Provided the mother is restored to the baby, or an acceptable substitute is provided, before the elapse of a critical period between the end of the third month of separation and the end of the fifth, then the disturbance disappears with striking rapidity.'[64] What is more important, no one had interpreted the statistics or emphasized that the individual responses are so varied. Of the 123 infants who were deprived of their mothers, 19 developed the now familiar 'anaclitic' form of depression, whilst 23 suffered reversible psycho-emotional disorders.[65] In other words, one third of them developed the fatal or serious disorders that everyone talks about. No one takes any interest in the 81 children who, having suffered the same deprivation, did not succumb to it. These children do not exist in the psychological literature because they were able to look after themselves.

Our culture puts the emphasis on unhappiness. Which does not mean that there is something morbid about our sensitivity to suffering. On the contrary, the fact that we emphasize the violence of emotional deprivation is an index of how civilized we have become. Perceiving unhappiness is a matter of perspective. In an environment where it is normal, we scarcely notice it. Just as it is tolerated or overlooked in violent cultures, violence becomes intolerable in societies in which it is no longer seen as a natural phenomenon. Our sensitivity to unhappiness is proof that our society demands happiness. Our refusal to tolerate violence proves that our culture no longer sees it as a value, or even as a necessary force.[66]

This moral attitude has a paradoxical effect. Because we only talk about unhappiness and put all the emphasis on the intolerable violence of the murders, rapes and torture that are committed all over the world, we have come to inhabit a world of verbal representations that consists essentially of the things we are fighting. Hence the feelings of disgust, indignation and sometimes relish that are triggered by our stories, films, novels and debates.

First meetings with survivors

Whilst it does concentrate on the survivors, research on resilience does not trivialize the seriousness of the trauma. It outlines a comparative method that allows us to steal a few ideas on how to survive, or even bounce back, from our resilient heroes.

Longitudinal and catamnestic methods appear to be well suited to collecting this kind of data. If we wish to estimate the overall effects of abuse, we have to compare the development of a group of children who have been abused with a similar population of children who have not.

When he wished to study the development of a group of privileged young people in 1938, Georges Vaillant came up with the bright idea of taking 204 eighteen-year-old students who had just been admitted to Harvard and monitoring them for forty-five years. Every two years the group's health, mental state and social development were recorded. Accounts of their progress through life were published from 1990 onwards.[67]

Twenty-three of the young men – there were no women at Harvard at this time – died before reaching sixty, including five who died during the Second World War. Eight students could not be traced. Thirty-nine men suffered major mental-health problems: there were eleven cases of serious depression, with despondency and loss of the will to live; six cases of emotional problems, with mood swings between euphoria and melancholia; twenty-two cases of serious mental illness, paranoia and hallucinatory psychosis. If the eight who could not be traced are included, this means that 23 per cent of the original group experienced mental disorders.

The findings of this fifty-year study tell us that, taking into account bouts of depression that were cured spontaneously, almost 30 per cent of a population of some of the most privileged young men in the world had difficult and painful lives.

If this study had simply ended by concluding that life is hard for everyone, it might have been difficult to justify the research budget. The authors therefore attempted to understand the positive defence mechanisms characteristic of those who had the happiest lives. The tests the subjects took every two years and the interviews carried out at Harvard made it possible to establish two very different populations. Vaillant analysed the 60 of the 204 subjects whose lives had been perfectly happy, and the 60 who presented the most serious psychic disorders. The researchers were surprised by two things.

The first was the realization that those who had had the 'hardest' childhoods (these were privileged young men) were those who had the most satisfying lives as adults, probably because, at the age of eighteen, their earlier ordeals had obliged them to mobilize positive defences. In contrast, those who had been overprotected as children were less well equipped to face up to the trials of life.

The second surprise was that the defence mechanisms most commonly noted in the adults who blossomed were the same as those observed in a population of resilient abused children:

- Sublimation: the life force is channelled into socially acceptable practices such as artistic, intellectual or ethical activities. This vitality, which derives its magnetism from society, allows wounded souls, both young and old, to avoid repression and to express themselves fully and for the benefit of all.
- Emotional self-control is associated with sublimation. There is no anger, despair, and no impulsive actions to satisfy immediate needs. The subjects have no difficulty in managing time and demonstrate an ability to defer the satisfaction of desires and to transform them in such a way as to make them socially acceptable.

Altruism was a characteristic feature of this population. Their devotion to others allowed these subjects to avoid inner conflict and to get others to love them by making them happy. The benefits are enormous; this is a good bargain.

Humour was also a valuable defence. When talking about it to others, their representation of the traumatic event allows the subjects to distance themselves from it, to be less damaged by their ordeal, and even to use it to their advantage by joking about it.

Almost 25 per cent of a population of abused children will, finally, experience lifelong recurrent depression. This very high figure is in keeping with the incidence of depression in the general population, and even in the privileged population.

So are abuse and depression unrelated? If we rely solely upon the statistics, there is a danger that we will arrive at this interpretation. The only way to explain this paradox is to learn to argue in terms of resilience. Both reparation and aggravation are possible at any given stage in the life of a child.

Our academic division of labour accentuates our professional bias. The clinicians describe the undeniable disorders they observe during the period over which they follow up the abused individual. But they do not know what happens to the individual once he or she has recovered. Clinicians know nothing about the positive solutions that are found by some abused children.

Saying that abuse does no long-term harm is quite out of the question. Abuse does a great deal of harm and forces the individual concerned to use the healthy part of his or her personality to defend him or herself and to become still more human.

The traps of direct observation: the fact that the outcome is successful does not mean that the process was painless

The immediate problems are surprisingly similar, whatever the culture and whatever the sociocultural level of the child's parents. Spectacular violence has less effect than the insidious emotional deprivation that is often associated with it. The world of these children is characterized by two intermingled themes: 'Why are they being aggressive towards me?' and 'Who could possibly love me?' The child's unhappiness fills every minute of her life, even when the abuser is not present. But very few clinicians take into account the fact that a child's character disorder can, in the long term, evolve because her personality is still developing, whereas it would be more constant if it were integrated into an adult personality.

In an attempt to defend themselves, children often display a combination of aggressiveness and precocious maturity. The two character traits produce behavioural scenarios that allow them to adapt to an environment that would destroy them if they did not have those defences. But their safeguards cost them dear. The aggression is not properly handled. A child who has been stabilized by an environment that makes her feel safe can allow herself to be trusting and knows how to retaliate when attacked, but a deprived child alternates between inertia, silence and numbness, and occasional outbursts of rage that are unfairly directed at those who are trying to love her.

The imaginary world of war children is full of houses being blown up by bombs and limbs being torn off; their drawings outline figures with red to represent blood and colour the corpses' clothes red.[68] What else could they do? Their imaginary world feeds on events to which they have been sensitized because they were exposed to them. For similar reasons, the imaginary world of abused children is populated by wicked adults, and they want those adults to love them. What we call sadism is a fascination, a secret enjoyment of the pain we inflict on those we love. For these children, inflicting pain is not really a pleasure because they immediately punish themselves for the satisfaction they get from it. They are in fact trying to prove to themselves that they are no longer the ones who are being abused. They are more interested in the hope of liberation than the pleasure of inflicting pain. The abused child's abusive scenario does not last long when their environment allows them to express themselves in other ways.

For years, little Serban had known nothing but the cold and hunger he experienced in a big sixty-bed dormitory in Transylvania. He was hit by adults who never said a word to the children and sexually assaulted by the big boys and the women cleaners. He reacted to the constant violence by lapsing into a state of prostration, emerging only to eat the plaster he pulled from the walls or to lick his shoes. When, at the age of twelve, he was taken in by a family in the south of France, he made astonishing progress. Within the space of a few months he learned the language. He was cheerful, enjoyed exploring the world around him and very happy at school until the day his teacher fell ill and was replaced by an adorable woman teacher. He fell under her spell, and immediately began to persecute her. This was his way of proving to himself that, thanks to the love he felt for her, he was no longer a child who had been bullied. It was his turn to be the bully. After being persecuted in the way that only a child can persecute an adult, his teacher ran out of the classroom to go and cry in the corridor, and Serban, who was reduced to despair by her tears, began to self-harm, just as he had done in Romania a few years earlier. A sadist would have enjoyed reducing his teacher to tears. Serban was reduced to despair and self-harm, so that only he, and not the woman he adored, was punished.

Serban now has a doctorate in philosophy and is still sorry he made the woman cry, but he would not recognize her if she passed him in the street.

This pattern is not unusual, regardless of what people say. Emotional disorders can be long lasting because such children want to seduce the adults who abuse them, and to abuse those whom they like. But the mechanisms of idealization and intellectualization come into play very quickly, and protect them. Paradoxically, taking them away from their parents makes them idealize them even more. They begin to dream of the perfect parents they would so like to have known.

Every Friday night Angelo's wealthy parents tied their ten-year-old boy to his bed so that they could go off for a weekend's skiing in peace. He got up to such mischief! When they got home on Sunday night, suntanned and happy, they would untie him, beat him and send him off to take a shower. He was so filthy! It was his little sister, who was, for her part, overprotected, who told the neighbours about this tragedy. Angelo was taken away from his parents and placed in care. Twenty years later, not only does he not take his revenge, he spends his Sundays repairing and looking after his parents' beautiful home. He hopes that by doing that, his parents will be overwhelmed by his actions and will love him at last. This emotional strategy allows Angelo to feel better about himself because it is a way of avoiding the hatred he feels, instead filling his inner world with delicious dreams. What he is building is not, however, a patio but a 'false self'. This is his way of building, in the real world, the inauthentic relationship he needs so badly. In order to compensate for the emotional deprivation he experienced as a child, he has become a mason, whereas he would have to face up to some basic problems if his true personality were to emerge.

Intellectualization brings more concrete benefits. Faced with an unbearably conflicting situation, the wounded individual makes an attempt to understand it. As Anna Freud remarks, 'When there is no danger, the individual can permit himself a certain degree of stupidity.'[69] But when we are faced with danger, we are forced to understand the aggressor: we will be better equipped to stand up to him. Wounded souls cannot avoid this kind of understanding, and 'readily turn their personal problems into global problems'.[70]

The quest for abstraction can sometimes be dangerous if it cuts us off from the world, or if a wounded soul uses it to humiliate someone who does not really understand what is going on. This form of defence is, however, so highly valued by our culture, and especially our educational system, that it is often very advantageous.

First, it restores us to emotional health. Children who were numb with unhappiness when they were being abused see no point in going to school because it means nothing to them and may even seem ridiculous. Compared with what lies in store for them when they go home at the end of the day, Pythagoras's theorem is just a joke. Learning the rules that govern the use of the past participle is ridiculous compared with the alcoholic violence of their fathers. But once an adult succeeds in knitting even the slightest bond with them, these children overinvest in school. Because clinicians simply make brief observations at the time of the abuse, they conclude that their unhappiness has reduced these children to a state of idiocy. Which is quite true. But once we get out of the laboratories and the hospital wards, and once we trace the development of these children as they tell us their life stories, we find that 'these young people put a lot of effort into their work at school'.[71]

When the family home is a place of horror, school becomes a place of happiness. It is at school that the child meets friends and adults who talk to her nicely. It is there that she plays at being socialized and enjoys learning. In such a context, school becomes a place of warmth, gaiety and hope. Some cohorts of abused children even do better than average at school.'[72] When it looks like a moment of paradise in a hellish day-to-day life, school becomes a place where a number of defence mechanisms can come into play at the same time: it provides emotional warmth, improves the children's self-esteem and promotes idealization, intellectualization, and activism. It allows them to hope they can take a material revenge by making money to counteract their misery, and that gives these children a morbid courage: getting qualifications becomes the balm that can heal all their wounds. 'I'm not very good at school, but I'm not afraid of work. Hard labour means nothing to me.

When I pass my exams, I'm going to become a social worker.' It is by no means unusual to hear an abused girl saying things like that as she tells her life story.

If these defences are to work, someone must lend a helping hand. The damaged child has to meet someone who can help her get back to knitting her life. That is why longitudinal studies make it easier to assess the development of damaged children and to arrive at a better understanding of how they have been able to restore themselves. The connotations of the notion of reparation, which is often evoked, are too legalistic, or even too mechanical, and the concept of restoration provides a better description of resilience. When a painting that has been damaged by water is restored, we witness a new birth, the emergence of a new beauty, and sometimes a metamorphosis. The colours are beautiful and fresh, but they are not always the original colours. The important thing is to understand what the picture looked like before it was damaged, and what has been done to restore it.

Knitting a sweater is never a linear process. Describing it can sometimes be a tortuous process. When, during the air raids on London during the Second World War, Dorothy Burlingham and Anna Freud studied the serious problems of their 'infants without families', they had no difficulty in establishing a cause-and-effect relationship between early emotional loss and the disorders that immediately followed: the children lost weight, were small for their age, had problems controlling their sphincters, and their language development was delayed.[73]

My answer to those who say, 'Early problems, lasting effects,' is that the early effects of early problems can be long lasting if the family and social environment turn them into narratives that never change

René Spitz and John Bowlby were the first to note the long-term effects of early deprivation. This way of thinking, which is common among psychoanalysts, is still not accepted by our culture, which often takes the view that 'all that's in the past', as though we have no memory and as though our history has no effect on our identity and the decisions we take. Margaret Mead took a very dim view of such claims, arguing that they were mainly a ploy designed to keep women in the home.[74]

Opinions are now more qualified. The Meudon crèche founded by Emile Zola and the foundling hospitals of the day were orphanages similar to those found today in Romania, Russia or China. Those who think that children do not need an environment in order to develop isolate them in big buildings and thus create a situation of sensory, emotional and social deprivation that makes it quite impossible for young children to become human.

As soon as children are given a few lessons in development, their progress is so spectacular that it is no longer possible to correlate long-term effects with early deprivation. This does not mean that no traces are left deep inside the organism or psyche of a child who has been abused. When, between 1950 and 1980, Serge Lebovici followed up twenty children who had been brought up by mothers suffering from post-natal depression, he found that they were very damaged and chronically depressed, that their development was arrested, and that all of them either committed suicide before they were thirty, or died in 'accidents' or from avoidable illnesses.[75]

These children experienced a catastrophic evolution because the pain their mothers were suffering surrounded them with the sort of emotional environment in which it was impossible for them to develop. When they and their mothers were hospitalized together from the 1970s onwards, their mothers, who now felt safe and stimulated, spontaneously recovered the ability to provide them with the development guidance they needed. From that point onwards, their development was no longer catastrophic.

We must, however, make a distinction between the direct effects of a trauma and the effects of how it is represented. Little Marie survived the terrible damage her mother inflicted on her when she threw herself out of the window with the child in her arms. Everyone was astonished by Marie's ability to recuperate, her cheerfulness and her ability to form relationships. And then one day she explained that she had been hanging out of the window and that her mother died because she tried to grab her. The direct effects of the trauma had been easily spotted by the generous environment into which the girl had so easily inserted herself. The high quality of her early interactions had already taught her how to knit bonds that made her feel both happy and safe. But as soon as she was able to understand what death meant, she blamed herself because she felt that her mother's world had revolved around her and that she was to blame for everything that had happened to her. Because the early bond had been properly woven, she was able to repair the direct effects of the tragedy. But the very fact that it was properly woven gave rise to the feeling that she was to blame for her mother's death.

The trauma was repaired thanks to the quality of her early interactions and thanks to the social organization that allowed the motivated adults to give her a helping hand. But the way the trauma was represented created a costly relational style until the damaged girl learned to use guilt to lend other damaged children a helping hand. This type of 'knitting' logic is much more in keeping with the astonishing variability we find in the clinical literature. Whilst it is true that all children suffer in both biological and emotional terms when their family environment is damaged, we find that those best equipped to recover are the children who come from privileged social backgrounds.[76]

But we can no longer argue in linear terms. We can no longer say, 'Children who have been affected by their degraded environment recover best if their parents have a good income.' If we base our argument on the notion of resilience, it would be more accurate to say, 'Whilst these children were affected by their chaotic environment, they could hold their own because the foundations of their personalities had already been solidly laid by a comfortable and reassuring family environment.' Which comes down to saying that certain social milieus can provide such a family background without having a fantastic pay packet. It is not only the direct effects of the trauma that have to be repaired; the effects of how the trauma has been represented must also be repaired. All too often, academic discourse says, 'You're finished. You were damaged during your early childhood, and science shows that the damage cannot be undone. What is more, you are the child of genetically inferior parents. Worse still, you have so many social handicaps that you have no reason to be optimistic.' So a trauma born of a social representation aggravates the direct effects of the trauma itself. The only difference being that, whatever our culture now tells us, a trauma's biological effects can often be repaired because the brain is so plastic. In contrast, the effects that can be attributed to an academic discourse can only be repaired if our social discourse can be changed, and that can take several years or even several centuries.

Early bereavement exacerbates both aspects of the trauma. When a child's emotional environment is destroyed because he has lost his parents, he has to make a huge effort to re-establish a few bonds. But when social discourse says of him, 'He's a poor orphan. He's finished. But, out of the goodness of our hearts we will take him into care and make a farm boy of him,' society puts an additional psychosocial obstacle in the path of his development. This twofold aggression may explain why children who lose their parents at a very early age are four times more likely to suffer from depression as adults than those who had an ordinary childhood.[77]

So what is it that blocks the development of these individuals? Is it the traces left in the brain by their early emotional deprivation? Or is it the social representations that used to give orphans an inferior social status? The neurological traces can be identified. Brain scans of Romanian orphans show that their ventricles and cortexes swell when they come back to life in their foster families. Is it possible that the relational disorders that result from isolation make it more difficult for them to become part of our culture? They can be rehabilitated if the institution thinks they can and teaches these children about their culture's rituals. All too often the damage inflicted by social discourses condemns these poor children and makes them become monsters, retarded or delinquent. The latter hypothesis is the more plausible because those children who were orphaned at a very early age but who do bond with an institution, a family or, later in life, a partner, prove to be no more depressed than the general population.[78]

Emotional vulnerability can be transformed into emotional strength, if we are prepared to pay the price

For individuals who have suffered deprivation, weaving this bond has an importance and an acuity that it does not always have for those who felt safe enough as children and were stabilized by their parents' affection. For them, emotional involvement is vital.[79] That is why we find that, after an adolescent period during which both the search for love and break-ups are common, their marriages are more stable than those of the overall population, once their choice of partner has been decided. From that point onwards, they can overcome their fear of life-long commitment. 'After the age of twenty-five, we find that the situation becomes more settled. This may be an indication that their person-alities have been consolidated and that they wish to alter their personal histories in order at last to have the partnerships that most of them did not experience as children.'[80]

Because they were emotionally hurt as children, these young people have been so sensitized to this type of bond that, after a period of anxious overinvestment which takes the form of a fear of commitment, we find that their marriages are stable, make them feel safe and give them greater strength. Conversely, a child who felt safe as his personality developed finds commitment easy because he finds the bond less oppressive. For the same reason, he will break off a relationship without too much difficulty, should the pressures of marriage require him to do so. Anyone who has been emotionally wounded is prepared to pay a very high price to preserve the stability of a bond that protects him. Such people are respected by a social discourse that sings the praises of couples who stay together, but would be despised by a discourse that places the emphasis on individual careers.

This example of how emotional vulnerability can be transformed into a form of strength at any cost is a good illustration of how resilience can be knitted. Wounded children can come into their own as adults but there is a price to be paid: their life strategies are appropriate, but they cost them dear.

When it comes to making the most important life choices – 'choosing a partner and choosing a career' – the quality of the emotional bond between these resilient young people depends upon how they are welcomed by their partners' personality and the degree to which it is culturally acceptable.

Because these young people invest so much in their emotional lives, they may be reluctant to commit themselves, which explains why they marry late.[81] If, however, their partners can tune in to this kind of emotional demand, their support becomes a major source of strength. Girls who have been brought up in institutions usually derive less satisfaction from marriage than those who haven't. If, however, we look at a sub-group of girls who have survived that ordeal, we often find that they have chosen attentive husbands who were prepared to help their future wives as soon as they met them.[82] The need for a 'supportive' husband was much less pronounced in traditionally raised young women, who more often succeeded in organizing their lives even when their husbands gave them no help.

When we try to understand how a partner supports his wife, we find that they are bound together by a sort of 'contract', a shared life-project, a mad dream that they need to fulfil, or a search for mutual re-assurance.

Throughout her childhood Léonie was humiliated

by her mother, who never missed an opportunity to tell her daughter that she was ugly, timid, bad at school, and that she would never make anything of her life; she took pleasure in humiliating her. Auguste had never been really unhappy as a child, but his parents moved around the country so much that he was never able to establish any ties of friendship. He always felt as though he was 'from somewhere else'. When he met Léonie, he immediately realized that he would become important to her and that they could settle down together in some pretty little town by the sea. The contract was sealed, and Léonie would say, 'When I'm with him I feel both beautiful and clever.'

Girls who were brought up in institutions and who are unhappily married have never entered into a marriage contract like that. They were so helpless and their self-esteem was so poor that they accepted the first offer that came their way. As one of them said, 'When you're drowning, you cling to any plank you can find.' That is what Séverine did. No one knew why she had been an anaclitic child in her own family. Her failure to thrive was associated with very poor language skills. The nervous way she constantly cleared her throat inflamed it. Once she was put into foster care at the age of about five she came back to life, put on weight and began to speak so fluently that, after doing brilliantly at school, she went on to do very well at university. Even though the way she caught up showed how resilient she was, her self-esteem was still so poor that she accepted the first marriage proposal that came her way. Even before he became her husband, Clément realized he would be able to live the life of Riley and that his 'little woman' would always do everything for him. Fifteen years later Séverine never stops working, looks after the house and never has a harsh word to say about her husband's gambling. 'I stay with him because he's nice to me from time to time. I don't love him any more, but I can't leave him.' Choosing a husband like this damaged her resilience badly, whereas those women who did succeed in finding supportive husbands always turned down the unsuitable candidates.

As soon as we choose a partner, social factors come into play. Almost all the women who did meet supportive husbands came from groups in which they felt safe, had lived in institutions that had succeeded in giving them a strong feeling of belonging, or had remained with their foster families well into their twenties.[83]

A feeling of belonging makes it easy to have a good sense of self-esteem because belonging to a group is all it takes to make one proud of belonging to it. Everything to do with the group is better than anything we can do as individuals. Belonging to a group is all it takes for stealing to become an initiation rite if all our friends are thieves, for commercial success to mean more than having a happy family, if that is the way our friends see it, and for the values of a different group to look ridiculous.

All human beings, whatever their culture, have to come to terms with the problem of the taboo on incest. They have to reconcile two needs that are both contradictory and closely associated: the need to belong, so as to feel they have support, and the need to become autonomous, so that they can feel proud of having won their freedom. The incest taboo is the linchpin that makes it possible to articulate these contradictory needs: it allows us to leave our family of origin whilst still remaining part of it. This emotional-social mechanism ensures that we remain at a safe distance from our families. But when an impulsive young man breaks away from his family of origin, he loses the security of belonging to a family, and when a young man who is not impulsive enough does not break away from it, he does not experience the pride that comes from becoming autonomous.

Young people who were once 'infants without families' have great difficulty in winning their social autonomy. Because they do not have the security of a feeling of belonging and have been badly advised by the culture in which they live, they feel a need to be self-reliant. And because they are uncertain of where they are going, they allow themselves to be influenced by those who judge them and who take a poor view of them. That is why, when they come of age, many young people without families ask to remain in touch with the social services and often go back to live with their foster families.[84] Because they have little support and are lacking in self-confidence, they find it difficult to move on; 30 per cent of them become passive welfare recipients and remain on benefits for the rest of their lives, and 30 per cent become unstable in both social and emotional terms. The casual jobs they take and their fleeting affections reveal their fear of commitment. They avoid the jobs they like and the women they love because they think that having their hopes dashed is less painful than coming to terms with the fact that they have no dreams for the future. The 30 per cent who do survive are not afraid to dream, and dare to love.

The most neurotic choices we make in our lives
— choosing a career and choosing a partner —
supply the theme of our lives; but every meeting
is a turning point, a sensitive period, and we
have to negotiate a compromise between our
subjective history and social discourse

As educational institutions come to have a greater influence on our children's life choices, and as more children are taken into institutional care, vulnerable youngsters will find it increasingly difficult to survive because a bit of disorder (or at least an absence of rigidity) leaves room for creativity. Yesterday's village idiots have become today's institutional idiots because our society takes so many of them into care. But 'more' does not mean 'better'. Perhaps we have to keep a safe social distance from institutions in the same way that the incest taboo helps us keep a safe emotional distance from our families.

The most neurotic choices we make in our lives – choosing a career and choosing a partner – are basically made when we are young, and youth is a sensitive period. Before we can look forward to a future that is structured by our dreams, our past must be structured by our emotional environment. At both these existential turning points it is our foster environment that supports and orients us. Young people whose childhood foster environment attached little importance to school and intellectual adventures tend to work in jobs that bring them into contact with other people (because they work with their hands or in the retail sector) and appreciate strong group loyalties. The choices made by children when their foster environment made a virtue of abstraction are more neurotic.[85] They tend to opt for artistic or intellectual careers, and the meaning of their life stories tends to be determined by the settling of family or social scores: 'I suffered too much because we were poor. I was too ashamed to go and ask the grocer for credit, and I was mortified at having to wear shoes that had holes in them. So I married a very brave man, and we took our revenge on my poverty and now I buy my granddaughter the most beautiful shoes in the world. My daughter tells me that I'm overdoing it, but I need to buy her lovely shoes.' The woman who told me about her wretched childhood was devoting her life to making her dreams of revenge come true with a morbid courage. Despite the generosity she displays when it comes to buying her granddaughter lovely shoes, intellectual and social success had become so important to her that she prioritized individual development over family solidarity. So much so that, when her business expanded, she had no qualms about going to live in the United States, far away from the daughter and granddaughter she adored. Her idea of family solidarity allowed her to leave her loved ones behind. Children who have been shaped by an environment that prioritizes context and emotional closeness never do that.

We can predict how these very different life strategies will evolve. There are those who believe in context, and those who believe in representations. Our culture now promotes the ideology of the self and places the emphasis on what we call 'social success', which actually means that the self is a social success. Sacrifice is no longer what it used to be. For our grandparents, the word had the glorious meaning of 'self-renunciation for the greater good of all'. It has changed so much that it has almost come to mean 'you've been had'.

Another part of our culture tends to prioritize the strategy of the immediate, but it is more discreet and rarely finds expression in our public discourses. For those who support this view, there is something shameful about success and something immoral about money. Geographical closeness and family solidarity are the only things that are worth mentioning.

It is the structure of the environments that foster us, before and after we become adolescents, that govern the existential choices we make. We can almost predict the emotional and social future of a population of damaged young people by looking at the values of the institutions that took them in.

In 1946, children's villages were built in France for those who had lost their parents during the war. Mégève and Villard-de-Lans took in over a thousand children. The Rhône-Alpes region paid a high price for the courage it had displayed in supporting the resistance: the parents of 10 per cent of the children in these villages had been shot. The 'orphans' village' was founded by de Croli (Brussels), G. Romanet and Yves Farges (Académie de Lyon). Its construction was financed by American and Swiss charities.[86] Had it not been for that institution, most of those children would have died, become encephalopathic, or ended up as long-term patients in psychiatric wards. At the time, the goal was to find new ways of caring for children without families, some of them very damaged. The adults structured the foster environment with the pre-occupations of adults who had forgotten the values of childhood. For the adults, the uniforms the children wore signified 'equality' and 'cleanliness', but for the children they meant 'everyone looks down on us'. The big blue capes, the berets worn at an angle and the shaven heads meant that these children were socially despised. Yet fifty years later, the few resilient survivors I was able to meet were amazed at how proud they were of having once had to wear the clothes that stigmatized them as orphans, and of having survived. In retrospect, the clothes changed their meaning, spoke a different 'discourse' and became proof that they had done well.

One of the staff's other preoccupations was to ensure that these poor children were not corrupted by the luxury of the requisitioned hotels they were living in. Once they had experienced the luxury hotels in a winter sports centre and the comforts of living in modern and well-equipped chalets, wouldn't they be disoriented and then embittered when they came into contact with real life? Not one of the children taken into these institutions has any recollection of the luxurious panelling, the big rooms or the beautiful chandeliers. Adult values which meant nothing to them could not even become memories.

This misunderstanding did not prevent the staff from defending the interests of the children in their care. When the resort's doctors objected to the creation of the village on the grounds that 'poor children' would be privileged at the expense of middle-class children who were really ill, and whose parents had to pay the institutions that took them in, the staff defended the children in their care by pointing out that they had made 'astonishing progress' and had 'caught up in terms of language development'. They pointed to the 'good mental attitude of these children, who are determined to overcome all the natural difficulties that the war has created for their families.'[87]

The foster environment can in fact be represented as a network, as a web that organizes the child's environment.

When he went into the home in Villard-de-Lans, the seven-year-old Michel had lost the power of speech. He constantly rocked backwards and forwards, and self-harmed whenever anyone attempted to relate to him. His progress was astonishing. Within a few months, he had caught up in terms of his language skills. He made everyone laugh with the little plays he made up, and had decided that he wanted to be a *chasseur alpin*: a soldier in the French mountain infantry. He had been told that his parents had been shot by the Germans. He did not dare say that he was proud of the way they died. And then one day, a tall, beautiful woman came to visit him. She was heavily made up, wore a blue dress and a big white hat. Michel's mother was not dead! She was living in Lyon and having a great time. As she left, she explained to the child that she could not take him with her but would come to see him again. That evening Michel relapsed into silence and began to self-harm.

The process of knitting his resilience got off to a good start when he was taken into the home. The secret pride he took in the way his parents had died gave him a certain self-esteem. Because he was in a favourable foster structure, he began to blossom. The institution's adult discourse said that you had to be kind to the children, toughen them up by making them walk in the snow and train them for manual work. Despite the privations that had damaged him, and which explained his self-centred rocking, Michel's inner world was coming back to life. One visit from his mother was all it took to change the meaning he ascribed to his ordeals. He was no longer the son of a heroine. A single visit was all it took to make him the abandoned child of a loose woman.

This example illustrates the extent to which human determinations work in the short term. If one row of stitches is well knitted, the next is easier, but any event can change the quality of the whole garment.

Some moments are, of course, more sensitive than others. Biological learning processes are at their liveliest when we are young; we give the people we love the power to influence us, and certain situations that are highlighted by social discourses can act as supports that help to socialize us, or as sets of points that marginalize us. We spend our lives knitting ourselves with biological, emotional, psychological and social skeins of wool.

Every meeting represents a turning point. Which is not to say that we are free to knit our lives as we see fit because, when we meet someone, we have already been shaped by our past and because the environment we use to knit ourselves is itself made up of its narratives, institutions, traditions and technologies.

Our choices of career and of partner illustrate how individuals use their environment to knit themselves. Our inner world can, however, change, depending on whom we meet. A child who is doing badly at school may overinvest in it if he meets an older friend, a good pupil who acts as a role model, or a woman teacher who, with just one word or one expression of admiration, can awaken a mind that has become dormant. The fact that most of a population of abandoned children will become delinquents does not mean that emotional deprivation leads to delinquency. It suggests, rather, that a society that goes on saying that 'any child without a family is a bad lot' organizes social pathways that lead children without families into delinquency. Kids in Bogotá 'steal whatever they can get their hands on. They get their kicks by hanging on to the bumpers of moving cars because, for them, stealing and thrill-seeking is a perfect way of adapting to their street culture.'[88] A street child who does not steal or live for kicks does not have a great life expectancy.

The gaze of others has the power to shape us

The way children who are brought up in an institution grow up reveals what that institution thinks of children. This general picture was confirmed when 164 questionnaires were sent out to former boarding-school pupils in an attempt to discover what had become of them after ten years.[89] They married late and were good at their jobs, which were usually chosen because they brought them into contact with other people (in, for example, the building industry and the retail sector). Those from underprivileged socioeconomic backgrounds found being autonomous more difficult than those with wealthy parents, and often (70 per cent) went back to live with their families of origin. Most (again 70 per cent) were quite content with their lives. There were fewer delinquents than in the overall population. They did less sport, were more likely to own motorcycles, and moved house less frequently. The way this small population developed shows that the efforts made by the social-work team were rewarded with success, and reveals how they viewed the children.

It is as though they had said to themselves, 'You have to be generous towards these children and pay them a lot of attention, and you have to be moralizing. But there is no point in being ambitious for them. They have enough problems as it is.'

An institution is structured like a personality. Its walls and rules are a material expression of how the people in charge think. Damaged children have to grow up in institutions like this, and with an astonishing variety of mentors.

The thousands of children whose parents were deported during the Second World War were taken into institutional care. Some of the children in care had themselves been deported.[90] The 'corrupting effect of luxury' was not a major concern for these people who ran the homes, which were very poor and very simple, and which were sometimes expanded by using surplus army tents. And yet the children in them did experience a kind of luxury.

It is estimated that 11,000 children died in the Nazi concentration camps, that 12,000–16,000 were brought up by relatives, and that 6,000–8,000 were taken into institutional care after the war.[91] And it transpires that it was the 'philosophy' of each institution that determined how they developed.

Seventy per cent of the children who passed through these homes state that they changed their lives. Many of them describe the encounters they had there as coincidences, but we now know that the 'coincidental' nature of our social encounters is very much determined by the subject's attitude towards his or her environment. Some self-centred children were too damaged to meet anyone. The adults had to take the initiative. But once they had warmed up and had come back to life, they were eager to meet anyone they could.

For most of them (55 per cent), meeting their partners was the most important happy event in their lives. The fact that they had some emotional support and felt stable at last allowed them to formulate a plan for the future. 'The gratitude I felt towards that strong older man . . . the young self-taught man I still admire . . . the beautiful, intelligent and strong woman without whom I would never have become the man I am today . . .' Because wounded souls have a bulimic need for affection, they overinvest in their partners. Individuals who have never been hurt would probably never be prepared to put the same effort into their relationships as these young people. That is how great their need for the affection of others was.

Some (31 per cent) also overinvested in their families, when there was anyone still alive. For 20 per cent friendship took on an importance that their friends could never have suspected. 'I decided to enrol in the Arts Faculty because I was friends with Marc at the time. His parents were teachers and they encouraged him to do an arts course.' For those children who had lost their families, it was the families of those they loved that determined the choices they made at this time. Teachers and work colleagues can also come into the category of 'the friends who saved me'.

For these children, some cultural heroes had such power that they helped to negotiate existential turning points: 'I spoke to Jean Marais, and he recognized me afterwards . . . François Maspéro confided in me, one night in Algeria . . . Klarsfeld, one night in Montreuil . . . My sister, who went with me, told me that she saw my face change.'[92] Youth movements, political and social commitments and evenings at the theatres gave these deprived young people some pleasant surprises.

Religion breathed new mental life into 9 per cent of these children: 'I found God in Lyon one evening . . . a representative of the Jewish community in Paris . . . my conversion to Catholicism . . . going back to Judaism . . .' The fact of not having been exposed to a family god as a child means that, a few years later, it is possible to find the God of all men rather than a domestic god.

Some institutions strongly urged their young people to go to university, whilst others neglected to do so, which reveals teachers' power to influence human souls. Even when they were not verbalized, their subjective values influenced the existential choices made by the children in their care.

The reasons we make the choices we make do not,

therefore, lie in the immediate, but in the private histories of wounded souls who, with varying degrees of success, integrate themselves into the collective history of the environments in which they live. We have to look to our environment and our antecedents to discover what determined our existential choices.

It is not enough to say that a good environment produces good children, or that a child who develops well in personal terms will become a well-rounded adult. What we are knitting changes with every stitch: a child whose development was satisfactory may collapse when he has to face up to his first existential ordeal if he has never had the opportunity to learn to survive the tricks fate plays on him. Conversely, a vulnerable child can make sense of her life by overinvesting in emotions, intellect, or in abstract concepts.

A child is a sponge that soaks up emotions. But no child simply soaks up whatever the environment has to offer. Her development and history sensitize her to particular kinds of environment, and she will seek them out. Her sensitivity is different at every stage because it is still under construction. The problems are always different, even though the subject's identity governs the way in which he experiences his world with its theme: 'No one loves me . . . I'm the man with the brooding good looks . . . It's not fair . . . I bring bad luck . . . Something wonderful is going to happen to me . . .'

The world may taste the same but we have to resolve the problems of our age in every chapter of our stories. Knit one stitch for our past and our subjective life, another for our culture and those who are close to us. That is how we knit our lives.

III

Memories as Stories

'All sorrows can be borne if you put them into a story'

'Once upon a time there was a little village girl, the prettiest that had ever been seen. Her mother doted on her. Her grandmother was even fonder ... she went by the name of Little Red Riding Hood.'¹ This is how Charles Perrault, writing in the seventeenth century, begins one of his fairy tales.

'In Alsace, round about 1850, a schoolmaster, burdened with children, agreed to become a grocer.'² This is how Jean-Paul Sartre begins his autobiography. He entitles it *Words* so as to make it clear that he does not intend to tell the truth and that he is going to turn what he believes to be his personal history into a story.

'I was born like a bitch and I've made myself a queen,' Madame M said to me when she came to tell me the story of her bitch of a life. Her mother died in childbirth. At the age of thirteen she was raped by her father. She was put in an institution where she suffered terrible abuse. She is now a rich business-woman. She went on: 'My beauty is a weapon, and so is my courage.' And then she explained that, in order to make better use of her weapons, she refuses to let herself feel any emotions.

We feel a strange need to turn our lives into stories.

Doing so is also a strange pleasure. 'All sorrows can be borne if you can put them into a story,' says the Danish author Isak Dinesen.[3] When we come face to face with horror, we feel both a need to talk about it and a need to keep quiet about it. If we talk about the disaster we have suffered, we make it exist in someone else's mind and delude ourselves into thinking that he or she understands us, despite the pain. We also turn our ordeal into a secret that takes the form of a relationship: 'You are the only one I've told.' Our ordeal undergoes an emotional transformation; once it is shared, it changes. It is the third party who creates the illusion of understanding, especially if that third party is far removed from us. If we are to be completely understood, the third party must be a pure representation. When we share someone else's day-to-day life, we know that he is mistaken, that he has too many sorrows and too many imperfections for us to trust him. A father (the one who took the decisions in the age of fathers), a master (he who knew everything in the age of masters) or God (who knows and sees all) is the perfect third party who can understand our misfortunes, the unhappiness we cannot admit to, and the prayer of our desires.

The ideal reader is also a perfect third party. As he is a long way off, he will not divulge our secrets. Because we idealize him, he will understand us perfectly, and the army of readers who read this book will include at least ten people who can understand and accept me, even though I have been hurt.

Once the anguish of making a spoken or written admission has passed, we often experience an astonishing feeling of calm. 'There you are. That's me. That's the way I am, and you can take it or leave it.' Taking on the identity of an autobiographer suddenly gives a feeling of coherence and acceptance. 'I've described myself as I am. From now on, those who love me will love me for what I am, and will accept what makes up my identity. I am the boy who . . . almost died . . . killed his mother as he was being born . . . was a delinquent . . .' Before I told my story, I got people to love me for the socially acceptable part of me, and I kept quiet about the other part of me. Now that I have told them my story and described myself, they love me for what I am, genuinely and completely.

This contract between author and reader is often signed; autobiographies sell very well. Every publisher is sent an autobiographical manuscript every other day, and hundreds of them are published every year. No matter whether the authors are celebrities like Elia Kazan, Françoise Dolto or Ingmar Bergman, or someone like Pierre Jakez Hélias,[4] whom no one had heard of until he sold two million copies of his book,[5] the books are all about day-to-day life, and turn the banal into something poetic. They are scenarios for popular novels, and the theme is always the same: 'No matter whether I am rich or poor, famous or unknown, I am going to tell you the story of my ordeals and how I survived them.' But it is only when the adult has truly blossomed despite his or her wounds that we realize that, fifty years ago, he or she was a resilient child. We have to interpret the past in the light of the present if we wish to give meaning to the events that occurred.

Zola, Hitchcock and Freud establish the rules of the genre

'This is a literature of the real and of intimacy,' writes Jean Malaurie, who would like to turn the genre into a Zolaesque literary naturalism.[6] Inspired by Claude Bernard's experimental method, Zola would go into workers' cafés or to farms and make a few rapid 'literary sketches': how people dressed, who did the talking and what was said, what the furnishings were, who slept in a bed and who slept on straw . . . ? And then, when he came to write his novels, he used these realist touches to imbue a social thesis with truth.[7]

When we tell our stories, we are all convinced that we are not lying, and think to ourselves: 'What a story! Extraordinary things have happened to me. I find them so fascinating that I'm going to tell you about them. Like me, you will be fascinated by it.' This simple formula immediately raises a problem. Why are all life stories structured like a film by Hitchcock? We see the tragedy coming, and sometimes we even know where and how it will unfold. The question that fascinates us is: how did the hero manage to survive?

Life stories are also structured like novels: we know that our hero became a famous singer and we also know that he was brought up in care or was a juvenile delinquent, so how did he get where he is today?[8] If he hadn't succeeded, it would just be an everyday tale about red tape or police stations. But because we know that he did succeed, the same story becomes a social fairy tale. It is the conclusion that gives past events meaning and transforms something unexceptional into something marvellous.

Freud emphasized that patients come up with superficial pieces of information that are meant to impress rather than aid understanding of their condition: 'The patients' inability to give an ordered history of their life insofar as it coincides with the history of their illness ... possesses great theoretical significance.'[9] It is true that most patients embark upon their psychological task by trying to imprint on the psychoanalyst's mind an image of themselves that will take a long time to fade. In day-to-day life it is even worse; people who are in therapy do at least know that no one is going to pass judgement on them. They are in a place where they can say what they think.

This attempt to impress has an important function: it is a deception that allows us to coexist by blinding us. If we always said whatever came into our heads, no couple and no group could go on living together. Brutality would be an everyday occurrence. If, on the other hand, we amputate one part of our personality, we can coexist quite happily. The 'handicap' then becomes a metaphor for life in society. But the deceptive self-image we implant in the minds of others works only because both partners – in the autobiography, the author and the reader – hope to share the same pleasure: 'I am going to tell you, in three acts, how I overcame tragedy in the course of my life' corresponds to 'He is going to tell us how he overcame his terrible tragedy, and his story will trigger a wonderful feeling of horror in me.' The oxymoron 'wonderful horror' is not a contradiction. The reader can experience a feeling of wonder while reading a horror story because the horrific events have a happy ending. Even though she was an incest victim, the French singer Barbara became a great artist.[10] Claude Rhodain is now a legal adviser to multinational companies, but at the age of seven he was abandoned on the platform of a disused railway station.[11]

The epilogue to the novel of a life is not death.

Death is nothing more than the end of a life, and the end of the story. The reason many first novels end with a death is that their authors have no imagination; death is an easy ending. Unlike the full stop of death, the denouement clarifies a muddled trajectory that concerns us all because such extreme circumstances might have befallen any of us. When the poor child becomes a success and blossoms, his past sufferings undergo a metamorphosis. The story of his misfortunes reassures us and gives us hope because the metamorphosis proves that he has won. Sailors, who are very good at telling horror stories, often tell deliciously terrifying tales that reassure their audience. The function of fear is to tame our emotions whilst giving us advice at the same time: 'The storm was so violent that I thought I was going to die, and then I suddenly realized that if I chopped down the mast with an axe, the hull would float without keeling over in the squall.' The horror has a reassuring effect because it supplies a code that tells us how to act in a dangerous situation. That is why autobiographies are like popular novels that give us hope. They are edifying: they teach us a lesson, and encourage us to be virtuous and constructive.

The 'autobiography' subject constructs the past in the light of the present. At the time of the actual ordeal, the wounded autobiographer can bear witness. But it takes the hindsight that makes sense of events to turn the story into an autobiography. After every

sexual assault she suffered, Claire Enjolet sought
refuge amongst the second-hand book stalls on the
banks of the Seine. She now teaches French, and her
trajectory helps us to understand the extent to which
literature helped her when disaster struck. 'I'm used
to dying. That's life . . . Life warned me what it would
be like, as far back as I can remember. Notre-Dame
is my chapel. The Seine's *quais* belong to me.'[12] It was
only after the event that she understood what the *quais*
of the Seine, the protective effect of Notre-Dame and
the booksellers had come to mean to her.

*A direct trauma leaves traces in the brain, but
these are reversible; our memories are therefore
stories told by people around us*

When we talk about our past we are not reliving it
but reconstructing it. That does not mean that we are
inventing it. It is not a lie. On the contrary, it is by
using elements of the past that we tell our stories.
But not everything that happens in our lives consti-
tutes an event. Our memories store only those things
to which we have been sensitized. In biological terms,
non-conscious pieces of information shape our brains
and leave traces that sensitize us to one type of event
rather than another. This is what happens with children who have been abandoned. If they have not been

abandoned for too long, they subsequently display an anxious hyper-attachment to people, things and places. If, however, they are left in emotional isolation for a long while they become indifferent to their surroundings.[13] The emotional deprivation they experienced as their personalities developed leaves traces, but no recollections. No one knows why children are so vulnerable to any emotional loss and so sensitive to any encounter. They often display real emotional bulimia. They do not remember the periods of isolation. 'I have no memories because I have no parents,' they say if they have not met any emotional substitutes who could reawaken their emotions.

That is the problem: we remember events only if they are charged with emotion. An isolated child eventually becomes numb and cannot remember anything because there are no events in her world for her to talk about. Similarly, an overprotected child becomes numb because her emotional confinement prevents her from perceiving events. Conversely, a child who has received adequate support recalls only emotionally charged events. Her responses to them may derive from those traces of her past that have sensitized her to certain circumstances, or from people around her who have stressed their importance.

Our primary memory is sensory; it leaves traces in the brain. On the other hand, the secondary memory that stores recollections that have been highlighted by those around us is inscribed in the long-term memory. It is sustained and constantly revised by the stories the child tells himself inside his head, or by the stories he tells others if his discourse has been socialized. Irrespective of whether we are talking about neuronal memory traces, which create a certain ability to experience events, or memories inscribed in private representations, it is always the environment that is imprinted on the brain. It is the environment that creates the inner world of the emotions and our inner language. Children without families who have been shunted from institution to institution have no recollection of the periods they spent in isolation. The stories they tell later are always about encounters and experiences that have been emotionally activated or rekindled. Which does not mean that they do not retain traces of the difficult moments.

Nine-year-old Bernard was one of the few children to survive Auschwitz. He was so emaciated that the doctors who examined him when he was repatriated commented out loud on his physical condition and were horrified by the way in which his pelvic bones protruded. Bernard's experience had left him emotionally indifferent. This became less pronounced when he got back to Paris and, although he had been living in an emotional desert, even he was surprised by the uncontrollable intensity of his newfound outbursts of joy, anger or despair. If we scan the brains of children who have been left in sensory isolation as a result of some social disaster we find that the limbic brain, which is the seat of memory and the emotions, has become atrophied. The atrophy can be reversed by the effects of the banal lessons of everyday life. In 1946 the gas encephalography technique was used to scan Bernard's brain. The scans showed the reversible atrophy of that part of the brain,[14] which goes some way towards explaining his lack of emotional control.

Another part of our emotions derives, however, from our representations. When the doctor who was examining him commented on the boy's protruding pelvic bones, little Bernard experienced a surprising feeling of tenderness and pride because the doctor's words reminded him of how his parents' bones had stuck out before they disappeared. Thanks to that image-representation (the hollow behind the protruding bones), the boy felt that he could inscribe himself in the lineage of his dead parents and that he had not betrayed them by surviving. 'I'm like them. I look like them. I am a continuation of them. I have not betrayed them. So I can survive without feeling too guilty about it.' Something horrible that had brought him very close to death had created in the inner world of the child's representations a feeling of tenderness and emotional pride. If, however, the child had talked about his inner world, his listeners would certainly have thought he was insane because his inner discourse was so out of step with their social discourse. After the war, adults silenced these children by telling them: 'We had to do without chocolate too, and what's more you've got someone to look after you. So you've nothing to complain about, you ungrateful kids.' The 'temptation of innocence' now makes it impossible to describe how the horrors Bernard had experienced triggered a discourse of tenderness and pride.[15] A normalizing and moralistic discourse now encourages us to churn out clichés about how anyone who has lived through such horrors should suffer for the rest of their lives.[16] To which another discourse replies: 'All that's exaggerated. The child probably caught mumps in the countryside around Auschwitz. It was very cold there.' A sequence of events that took place in the real world imprinted on the child's memory a few unspeakable representations that are quite divorced from public discourse.

It must, however, also be pointed out that what feeds into Bernard's memory is not his day-to-day suffering but the way he 'stages' his past. I say 'stages' because he has chosen elements of real events from his past and used them to write a play. He wrote it for himself, and it is performed in his inner language. He has metamorphosed his sufferings into a work of art, into a subjective stage play.

Had Bernard written down the things that filled his days in Auschwitz, he would have described the biting cold, the pangs of hunger, the torture of being beaten and the expectation that he too would die like his parents before him. Even in that dreadful context there were brief moments of happiness: the extra spoonful of watery soup he was given by a stranger, the contact with another human being that gave him a moment's warmth, the need to understand and the astonishing flashes of beauty in the obscene world described by all those who have gone through ordeals like this. Those were the events that punctuated his day-to-day existence.

What remains after the event are, however, the images which, in a different context, have acquired a different meaning and a different function. Bernard had to turn himself into an image or a story of what had happened to him. When it became possible to do so, he then had to turn it into a narrative that could be addressed to others. It was no longer the cold or the fear that took on a meaning in Bernard's memory. It was not the blows – which to many proved fatal. It was his protruding bones that became meaningful. In the story he told himself they meant: 'I am stronger than death, and I did not betray my parents.' In the same way that an advertisement uses an image and a few words to put over a lot of content, the semanticized image (the protruding bone) was becoming an integral part of his narrative identity, rather as though he were saying: 'I am the boy who underwent death and triumphed over it. I am right to be proud and strong, despite my terrible wounds.' That subjective discourse cannot, however, be communicated. Thanks to these images, the child can understand something that he finds difficult to translate into words. For an adult, a world of such contrasts is inconceivable.

The case of little Bernard teaches us that the events he lived through would simply have overwhelmed him with data if he had not been able to organize them and give them meaning by putting them into a story. But our history changes, depending on whether we address it to ourselves, to a woman we are trying to seduce, to a family we want to keep or to a current of opinion that can understand only one type of normative-moral narrative.

A life is not a history. It is a constant resolution of the problem of adaptation. But human life forces us to turn it into a history in order to avoid reducing it to a series of defensive reactions that allow us to survive. If, like Ana Novac, who was imprisoned in Auschwitz at the age of fourteen, little Bernard had made notes every day, he would have recorded a series of contextual but unconnected events, and not a narrative.[17] He would have described how a wretched existence could represent the strange and painful happiness of survival. How can we say to any normal human being, 'I almost died of hunger, from the blows I suffered and from the endless misery, but I was proud of the way my pelvic bones stuck out. That made me feel proud'?

The past is never simple. Before little Bernard could

see that the protruding pelvic bones of his horrifically thin body meant that he was his parents' child, he had to be able to live in a world of representations. And in order to do that, he had to have a memory and an environment. He had to be able to compare his protruding bones to those of his parents, and to say to himself in his inner language: 'My bones stick out just like theirs ... I am like them ... I can identify with my parents thanks to the image of them I keep in my memory. I loved them. I did not betray them, because I am still what they used to be. I am a continuation of them.' This feeling of being part of a lineage, which was a product of the horrors he had experienced, inspired in him a sense of loyalty that taught him to be proud of himself in an obscene world.

It cannot be said that a psychic assault automatically results in psychic damage. We can say that an assault can cause damage, depending on the meaning it acquires in our past and for those around us. Faced with the same violence, we all experience different feelings because we all have different family and social contexts and histories. Our feelings are emotions that are triggered by representations, and the nature of those representations depends upon what has been historicized in our memories. If little Bernard had not known his parents before the assault, there would be no trace of them in his memory, and the protruding bones would have been meaningless because he would have been unable to compare his bones with those of his parents. If, conversely, his affection for them had been suffocating, the bones would have taken on a different meaning: 'I am like my parents, but I really wanted to be different from them. I hate the way my bones stick out because it makes me look like them.' Had the violence gone on longer, Bernard would once more have been forced to react to immediate stimuli. Suffer less, protect yourself as best you can, swallow a little water, keep on breathing. But in such cases, protruding bones usually take on an unspoken meaning which the child secretly revises in his inner world but never expresses. It was the people around him who silenced the boy: 'You've got nothing to complain about. We didn't get white bread during the war either.' All the child has left is the story he tells himself. It is like a secret or, rather, something unspoken that develops deep inside him, even though he cannot express it clearly. The splitting of his personality is largely attributable to the reactions of those around him.

Some children who emerged from the camps were taken in by institutions whose discourse gave the same violence a different meaning: 'You were all skin and bones. You looked like your parents when they disappeared. You were always rocking. You bit yourself when anyone spoke to you. And now look at the progress you have made. You can talk. You can study. You will have to be very brave to make up for the death of your parents.' In institutions like this, the splitting became less pronounced in months.[18] When they were given the opportunity to do so, the children told their stories and that was all there was to it. But they rarely had that opportunity because few adults could understand such stories. Many of these children therefore became novelists or actors or worked in other fields that allowed them to tell stories that were both similar to their own and socially acceptable. For them, art became a suture, a way of stitching together those aspects of their personalities that had been torn apart. We can always talk about ourselves, provided that we never say 'I'.

The urge to speak makes it possible to write an autobiography without ever saying 'I'

What else can we do? The urge to talk about our lives inevitably finds ways to express itself. And when the subject cannot put it into words, he or she finds other means of expression, such as a commitment to women who have (like me) been raped, to helping children who have (like me) been physically abused, or, more simply, the expression of banal opinions that actually let slip a piece of personal information: 'I like bad, over-watery soup (like the soup we were given when I was in care, and I'm surprised to find I like it)', or 'I often think of that sequence in Truffaut's film *Les Quatre Cent Coups*, where the boys run away from the crocodile and hide in doorways (exactly the same thing happened to me near the cirque Médrano and the rue des Martyrs)'.

All opinions are autobiographical because they reveal our sensitivity to the world, but it is our environment that sensitizes us to one particular kind of information. That is why, when Sartre begins his autobiography with the words 'In Alsace, round about 1850, a schoolmaster, burdened with children, agreed to become a grocer', he is saying – very elegantly – what we all say when, in order to talk about ourselves, we say, like Georges Perec: 'I was born on Saturday, 7 March 1936, towards nine in the evening, in a maternity clinic located at 19 rue de l'Atlas, in the XIXth arrondissement of Paris.'[19] The first piece of information we give about ourselves begins with an event that cannot be inscribed in our memories because we were told about it by some social organization. Sartre begins his life story with a statement that was made by his family and filed away in the archives. Perhaps it is true. But perhaps it is a lie, a pseudo-message,[20] an imitation or a statement made by someone else that we have borrowed. No matter whether they are true or false, autobiographies always begin with memories that are external to us.

The relational aspect of memory is characteristic of all the stories we tell about ourselves. When

Georges Perec first attempted to immerse himself in his past in order to write *W, or The Memory of Childhood*, he could not finish the book because the experience was so painful. Dissecting the disappearance of his parents hurt too much, and the book is dedicated to the vowel 'E' (= *eux* [them], in other words his dead parents). Even saying that hurt: the best he could do was dedicate a book about his childhood memories to a vowel that evokes his parents. But the lonely evocation of an image, a photograph or a real memory made him aware of the pain of a permanent state of mourning because he never said goodbye to them. That never-ending pain, which was drowned out by his day-to-day activities, returned when he was alone with it, and when he spent hours looking at a photograph of his father.

And yet even the recollections that are buried in our memories were traced by someone else's emotion. Even numb memories are relational. 'For years I thought that Hitler had marched into Poland on 7 March 1936. I was wrong, about the date or about the country, but that's of no real importance. Hitler was already in power and the camps were working very smoothly.'[21] Georges Perec begins his autobiography with some contextual memories and administrative information that is so detailed that it borders on the absurd: '7 March . . . nine in the evening . . . maternity clinic located . . . XIXth arrondissement'. But these pointless details take on a meaning when they acquire social connotations: 'For years I thought [that it was the day] Hitler had marched into Poland.' It is as though Perec were associating the contextual memories of his date of birth with the invasion of Poland in order to tell us: 'I was born under the sign of death. My date of birth is hallmarked with the meaning those around me ascribed to the event of my birth: persecution.' That false memory speaks the truth.

It is hard, being sentenced to death at the age of six. When a child accepts that he has been sentenced to death he behaves in a resigned manner that looks strangely like risk taking: lost in his thoughts, he crosses roads without looking, happily dives into rivers where there are whirlpools and attempts climbing feats that are beyond his abilities. Melancholics are very familiar with this curious effect: they are alone and tortured by the imminence of living but feel calm once they begin to plan their own deaths. The simple behavioural scenario of hoarding drugs and writing their wills allows them to say to themselves in a non-verbal way and by using the few objects they have to hand: 'So there is a way out of my suffering.' The familiarity with death that calms melancholics and children who are under a death sentence is very different from the compulsive risk taking we see in overprotected children. Young children in care gamble with death by staging very spectacular ordeals, and the psychological effect of those ordeals allows them to prove themselves through risk taking.[22] 'I know my own worth now that I'm brave enough to fight the police who are responsible for keeping order after a football match.' This use of theatrical ordeals to shape the emotions explains the extraordinary splitting we find in sober civil servants, hard-working students and rich antique dealers who suddenly turn into hooligans who will stop at nothing. For their part, deprived children put themselves to the test in secrecy. They have no need of witnesses, but their familiarity with death allows them to say to themselves: 'If death wins, that's only natural. But if I survive, it must mean that I am stronger than death.' It is because they are resigned to their fate that such children experience an overwhelming serenity.

Children who have actually seen their families being killed and who expect to die in the very near future are often saved by an inner compulsion: 'For years I put off telling the tale ... Today, impelled by a commanding necessity and convinced that the events to which I was witness must be revealed and brought to light, I resolve to defer it no longer.'[23]

That is the most common form of resistance found in children who have been exposed to violence. That is why persecution is the best way to reinforce convictions.[24]

When our story becomes an emotional statement, the listener will be either moved or embarrassed by it

This story must, however, be addressed to someone who is prepared to hear or read it. At first, the story of the disaster means that the child has no cultural existence: 'You were sentenced to death when you were six . . . between the ages of ten and fourteen, you were raped by your father . . . you were a delinquent because you were living on the streets.' Only the child's inner language can understand these words. The immediate benefit is that they play a part in the construction of the child's identity: 'I am the boy who . . .' But this identity is a secret, marginal identity that cannot be talked about, and it causes the child's personality to split: the transparent, social part of it, which is often cheerful, masks a darker part that is both secret and shameful. The very fact of talking or writing about it can bring together the two parts of the divided ego. Georges Perec experimented with this idea when he wrote *Je me souviens*, a curious book made up of 480 sentences, each recounting a banal memory: 'Memory 35: I remember the Cerdan–Dauthuille match . . . Memory 44: I remember Jean Lec's broadcast . . . Memory 54: a magazine called *Le Grenier de Montmartre* . . . Memory 62: I remember *scoubidos* . . . Memory 142:

I remember that Alain Robbe-Grillet was an agronomist . . . Memory 382: I remember Picasso's dove, and his portrait of Stalin.'[24]

We have all played 'I remember'. It makes us feel euphoric, and the explanation for that is that we are exchanging memories and that sharing our daily lives leads to conviviality. At the 1988 Avignon Festival the actor Sami Frei appeared in a one-man show adapted from *Je me souviens*.[25] As he pedalled away on his stationary bicycle and recited 'I remember . . .' every memory reminded everyone in the audience of some past event: 'It's true, I remember that too.' Sharing banalities like that created an astonishing feeling of emotional closeness amongst everyone who had experienced the same 'I remember's.

If we share the same memories, the mere mention of past events can even help us to control our emotions: 'Do you remember when we went and stole some of that yellow or blue liqueur from your dad's drinks cabinet and added a bit of water to keep the level the same?' We feel a tenderness for people with whom we have shared the same ordeals: 'Do you remember when he used to buy a baguette to mop up the sauce from the little tin of sardines that was all we had to eat?' It is easier to accept other people when they are willing to listen to our story. Even when we have not been part of the same events, we create a shared history and future memory as soon as we confide in each other. It is the beginning of an intimate relationship.

Talking about things is a way of experiencing them again, but in a different manner. It brings back the emotion we attributed to the event, but it is no longer the emotion we felt at the time because it has to be evoked and reshaped before it can be addressed to someone else, or shared with a listener or reader. Confiding in someone weaves an emotional bond, and that explains the intensity of the attachment that follows. 'I've never told anyone else what I've just told you. And now I am at your mercy. No matter whether our closeness is based on love or hate, I've put my life in your hands.'

When we tell our stories, we are taking a big risk. The words we use to describe our lives do not form an unemotional monologue or a simple checklist of objects or events. What is at stake in our life stories is of enormous political importance: our stories are designed to save Narcissus. They have the major emotional effect of weaving a bond of intimacy with the listener. And, more importantly, they put an end to the splitting. It is as if the speaker is saying, 'So far, I have expressed only the transparent part of myself, or what the conventions of our culture see as the most sociable part of me. I used the lovable part of myself to make people love me. And I kept quiet about the painful part of myself . . . It's not really secret; I just left it out. Now that I'm revealing my whole story, I'm asking people to love me for what I am.'

It is possible to hear an emotional statement like that and to be moved by it. It is also possible to be embarrassed by it. These are completely different relational strategies. Liking someone else's life story means accepting an intimate relationship that exists through the intermediary of a story or book. Conversely, those who say they are embarrassed by confessions and find them offensive ('it's like seeing him naked') are telling us that the only relationships they are interested in forming are socially sanctioned ones. They protect themselves from an intimate encounter with the author by hiding behind the conventions of social stereotypes. 'I' exist only because 'they' exist. When the ego is fragile, we use 'we' as a prosthesis. Framing our identity in this way is not unpleasant, as it allows us to commune as we worship the same idol and recite the same litanies. But the individual has the right to express himself only to the extent that he is a member of that community. The feeling of belonging is delicious, but it results in the loss of individuality and teaches us to despise those who worship different idols or recite different litanies.

Narcissus finds it very comforting to talk about himself. He feels like a fully rounded individual who, as almost always happens when an individual blossoms, is talking about the sufferings society inflicted upon him: 'I hate generals, judges, cops and priests because they justify the social edifice that hypocritically protects my father,' wrote Joël Arès. Arès is now an academic and writer, but he had a terrible childhood; he lost his mother and was raped by his father.[26]

The choices made by those who like autobiographies and those who do not like them reveal that they have adopted very different existential-political strategies. Some people enjoy intimate relationships and take little notice of social pressures whilst others feel comfortable only when they are within an institutionalized framework.

Any intimate memory is an encounter that has been socialized twice. When it is first socialized, our memory is impregnated by the environmental conditions at the time. It is then resocialized for a second time by another event, which can only prompt a recollection if it is given an emotional charge by who or what is around us. Children who grow up in isolation have no recollections, but their isolation does leave traces in their brains. And adults who are on beta-blockers or anti-depressants do not elaborate memories so long as they go on taking those substances because they dull their emotions.[27]

Only when we become adults can we choose from our past the significant events that become meaningful in the light of what we have become, and depending upon the person we are addressing. Any memory is a dialogue between what our environment has implanted deep within us and what we want to reveal about ourselves to others. A story is a verbal representation that recounts a series of significant events. Telling our story creates a coherent feeling of selfhood. It reconciles the two parts of the divided ego. The socially acceptable ego can at last tolerate the secret ego that cannot be talked about. The subject can at last talk about himself and express himself as a totality. It is as though he were saying: 'The blow I received made a painful part of my personality shrivel up. I could only express the healthy part, the part others could hear about without feeling uncomfortable. I am now a rich craftsman, writer or lawyer. Because the way I have been repaired is socially accepted, I can distance myself from my secret and become a sovereign individual. I can at last express my personality. As soon as I become whole, simply by describing what happened to me, I can face other people. I am no longer divided into a transparent part and a ghost-like part.' Now that it has been socialized twice, the memory of what we once were feeds into our story, which is itself an encounter, a negotiation between the speaker and the person who is listening.

When our memories play tricks on us, we remain prisoners of our past, as though we are suffering from post-traumatic stress disorder or have been brainwashed by propaganda

The slightest thing – a word, an image or an idol – can distort our memories when we try, as we must, to make them part of history. Post-traumatic stress disorder provides the most eloquent example of how this can happen. For years, the wounded soul revisits the scene of the tragedy every time he lets his guard down. It's like a waking nightmare, and any attempt to talk about it is almost always silenced by his culture. And so, the victim submits to a secret pain that gnaws away at him, and no one knows why he is tired, insomniac and irritable, or why he has so many mysterious ailments.

Any history is a product of social negotiations. But a subject who suffers from post-traumatic stress disorder is innocent. It is the environment that makes him distraught and imprints itself on his memory.

Private memories are meant to care for and identify wounded souls. 'I am the boy who saw his parents being tortured in front of him in Chile. One day, sometime in the future, I'll get my revenge on their torturers.' He is right to defend himself, but it takes only one encounter or a single word for him to use his history to influence others, to make others feel guilty and to justify taking revenge on moral grounds. As for the group to which he belongs, it almost always turns his tragedy into a tool it can use to manipulate public opinion. If that happens, his history becomes a justification or an edifying demonstration. It becomes a lesson in political morality or a programme for future action that can be hidden behind the alibi of the past.

The intentional aspect of public memory is beautifully illustrated by the way all those who seek power try to control those who manufacture history: 'The Church decided to introduce a system of censorship as soon as books, thanks to the development of printing, began to pose a threat to its teachings. In 1622, the Roman curia invented the neologism *Propaganda fide* to ensure that certain visual, historical and narrative techniques could allow the faith to be propagated. Napoleon tried to control writers so as to ensure that they described only the status of the citizens created by the Emperor. At the beginning of the twentieth century the Socialist Party thought that Christianity was a thing of the past, but used Christianity's techniques in an attempt to take its place.'[28] Nazism declared that literature must have only one theme: respect for tradition: '[a]n understanding of the uneven history of the intellectual and material development of the traditions of our ancestors can open our eyes and give us a keener sense of what does and what does not conform to our nature.'[29] The Soviet aesthetic wanted films that told how the brave man of the people freed himself from the chains of capitalism, and the Central Committee inspired the books that merited publication. In Algeria today, the most persecuted writers are those whose stories differ from those told by the men who want power. Totalitarianism relies upon the story of the past. When history is used in this way, it often means that someone is planning a vendetta. If we excavate the past we will always uncover something that cries out for vengeance. Forgetting the past is no solution; if we forget it, it will repeat itself. But if we submit to the past, we are getting ready to take our revenge. Forgetting the past might allow it to be repeated, but the manipulation of memory means that someone wants it to be repeated.

We can neither forget the past nor use it: the only solution is to understand it. In order to feel coherent and at ease with themselves, wounded souls must turn their ordeal into a story they can tell to a society which, having silenced them, is now prepared to praise them so as to turn their story into an ideological weapon or a bargaining chip in social negotiations. From the moment the story is told, listeners will begin using it to embroider social myths that suit their own purposes. The subject's memory stores recollections of the emotionally charged human context in which the event occurred. But, as soon as he has turned it into a story, all personal control over his history is lost, and the story feeds into a discourse he does not recognize. He has to talk about his sufferings in order to defend himself, he is talking to a culture that is constantly changing and which ascribes a meaning to those events that is very different from his own.

There are peoples with no history, and they are no worse than any others. The *bigoudens* live in the Pont-l'Abbé area of Brittany, but do not know where they come from. Gypsies, whose mother tongue has no written form, describe their past visually by arranging certain objects in ritual patterns, though they do not understand their meaning. Basques can exploit a poetry born of their mysterious language and origins. And for most such cultures there comes a time when its history ceases or fades into oblivion in the space of a few generations.

The Jews, in contrast, are the classic example of a people with a history. It is so tangled up with the history of other peoples that a historical atlas is required to understand it. They speak all sorts of languages and wear all sorts of costumes. Their origins lie in the history of a migration that took place 3,000 years ago. Having left Ur of the Chaldees because they rejected the custom of child sacrifice, the Jews settled in the Land of Canaan in Palestine. They adapted and left their mark on all the civilizations that came after them: Babylonian, Persian,

Greek, Roman and Byzantine, Arab and Ottoman, before becoming deeply involved in modern Western and Middle Eastern cultures.[30] Their example demonstrates the extent to which an understanding of one's past does not prevent it from being repeated. When other cultures know nothing of that history, they submit to a myth and force it upon the Jews.

When the act of remembering petrifies the future, and when control over the past reveals a totalitarian project, it becomes impossible to bear witness

The manufacturers of myths use their stories to sculpt a sort of cultural totem pole with which the group can identify. They make a perverse use of history to fabricate clannish bonds. The Americans invented rustic cowboys and sympathetic Unionists. They used fragments of real history and covered up anything that might embarrass them to ensure that all immigrants could identify with that chimera.

Even more so than forgetting, the abuse of memory petrifies the future and forces us to repeat the past. If we attempt to understand history and not to use it, we can associate memories that confer meaning with a disobedience to the past that encourages innovation.

Until recently, Western societies attached little importance to memory. The recent appearance of ancestor worship in the West is probably politically motivated. The return of Clovis in France, the Northern League's use of the old name 'Padania' in Italy, and the discovery of Canaanite pottery in Jerusalem and of a 9,000-year-old Caucasian skeleton in the United States are emblems that appear to say: 'Go away, we were here first.' Which is probably true. The problem lies in defining who 'we' are; if we do not know who 'we' are, we do not know who has to be driven out. The skeleton found by the Columbia river in the United States was that of someone who was Caucasian, and therefore light skinned. So all the Native Americans should leave. When it is used to plan the future, the past invents an ideological grammar.

It is the constant plasticity of the social body that explains this absurd logic. The 'we' is clearly identified for a few years, or for the time it takes to establish a cultural current. A social identity made up of a bundle of conflicting loyalties remains true for only a brief moment. Change is the only constant. Wounded souls, on the other hand, carry their wounds around with them in their memories. They are part of their individual identity. We change slowly as we grow older, but a cultural current can dry up or reverse the direction of its flow quite suddenly. In the course of a single biography we can therefore be carried away by shifting cultural currents. In 1946, a Polish Catholic reached the United States. He had been cruelly treated by the ideology of the Third Reich, which had taken away both his blond children so that they could be brought up by good Aryans. At the time, there were lots of Polish-language papers that would publicize stories like this. He was able to bear witness. The Polish newspapers no longer exist because the immigrants' children speak only English. But there are now a few universities where students sit their exams in Spanish in order to get American qualifications, and Asian schools where any student who associates with Westerners is accused of 'trying to pass for white'. The old Pole's wound has not healed, but he is forced to remain silent. No one understands him any more.

How can we describe our misfortunes in such a way as to paint a rounded self-portrait, and to give others a true picture of ourselves, when the culture of our listeners is constantly changing and altering the meaning of events? When Primo Levi returned from the death camps in 1946 and tried to bear witness, his book *If This Is A Man* sold 700 copies, even though he was already well known as a chemist. We can assume that only his friends and relatives bought his book. A sudden cultural change occurred in 1987: Europe developed a taste for stories of this kind, and almost 100,000 copies of his book were sold.

In the years following the Second World War deportees returning to France were silenced. There was a danger that their incongruous tales would spoil the party and poison the joyous renaissance of the French nation. Their eye-witness accounts would have put paid to the country's hopes. Which is why Holocaust denier Robert Faurisson did not find it too difficult to persuade the University of Lyon to accept his negationist thesis in 1971; it annihilates their memories by denying the existence of the death camps and the gas chambers.

Silence is the outcome of a cultural complicity that suits everyone's purposes. The deportees denied their own past so as not to have to reopen old wounds. They hoped that, by doing so, they would revert to being just like everyone else. 'What are these tears? What does it matter? Life goes on,' said Barbara.[31] The return to integrity is no longer possible. Any disaster forces us to undergo a metamorphosis because the only alternative is to keep the wounds open and to perpetuate the obscenity. Our metamorphosis means that we suffer less, like a wounded man who refuses to be moved.

All cultures are tempted to deny the past. Not a lot is said about the attempts to deny what happened during the 1914–18 war. The horror was such that the governments of the day decided not to talk about it so as not to perpetuate the nightmare: one and a half million dead, four million war veterans with severe facial injuries and five million cases of incurable illness.

Almost every family was either in mourning or caring for an invalid at home. And they had to keep quiet!

Even though Henri Barbusse's novel *Under Fire* had won the Prix Goncourt in 1916,[32] it was not until 1921 that a report by Louis Marin, who was *député* for Nancy, put an end to the negationism. Veterans' associations were founded and they erected war memorials in every village in France. The memorials were at once simple and commanding, and they meant that people could read the names of the local butcher and the peasant from the next farm rather than those of the generals and the officers. They allowed the little people and the humble to take their revenge. They had come face to face with the horrors of the war, and attempts had been made to silence them. 'These memorial ceremonies were not official government occasions. They were organized by veterans' groups.'[33] The government's negationism was a way of saying: 'Go away and die. Your suffering is an embarrassment.' But the worm turned. The veterans wrote about how they had suffered.

When the real is a source of embarrassment, society tries to deny its existence. People mocked the veterans' meetings, and the men were once more silenced. When they attempted to bear witness, men who had come back from hell were greeted with laughter. The Algerian conflict, the so-called 'policing operation' mounted by France in the 1960s, was another war that was never talked about. It had to be relativized for political reasons. For emotional reasons, many people living in metropolitan France believed that the army had either gone on holiday to Algeria or was defending the interests of the settlers: this was an attempt to deny that three million French soldiers served in Algeria, that there were 25,000 dead, a million wounded and thousands of people who 'disappeared'.

Unlike emotional denial, the attempt to control what we remember is a sign of totalitarianism. The denial of reality was the rule in the 1950s when, with communism at its height, intellectuals refused to listen to the eye-witness accounts of the Gulag, of trials in which there were no defence lawyers, of the purges, and of anti-Semitism in the USSR. If the theory is to be coherent, the information that obliges us to change it has to be blacked out. Order reigns in the world of representations. The real world is elsewhere.

In order to savour the pleasures of racism we have to be unable to put ourselves in the position of others, and must surrender to the mythical story known as 'collective memory'

Emotional denial is like a wounded man's denial that he has been hurt; it is a defence mechanism and it alleviates our suffering. Negationism, in contrast, is intentional. It is a discursive attempt to annihilate, and a prelude to actual annihilation. Psychological denial allows us to have a pleasant evening, but the intentional use of forgetting is a way of experiencing the pleasures of racism.

Racism really is a form of pleasure. When the German film maker Leni Riefensthal filmed the 1936 Berlin Olympics, she was – without, she says, realizing it – producing Nazi imagery. The young people were good looking, blond and looked to the sky. The light made their muscles stand out. Their constant victories procured them a carnivorous joy because they were victorious over other races. All films of this kind semanticize their images by making them tell of order, hierarchy, purity, strength and ancestry. The crowds stood to attention as the winner mounted the floodlit podium to commune with the founding fathers of the race. At the same time, communist films associated the might of military parades with the friendly disorder of the brave proletariat and their little father.

In both cases, the totalitarian theatricality and the orchestration of crowds were used to construct narrative images that implied negationism. All conflicting accounts had to be suppressed if the picture was to be clear and convincing and prove what it set out to prove. Any debate would blur the image and, by making it more balanced, make it less convincing. Doubts prevent us from being happy. Democrats are

people who break spells. They do so by showing us
that blacks are more than just good dancers, and that
they can discuss art and philosophy as well as white
people can. They make white people's sentimental
rhetoric stammer. The rhetoric teaches whites that
they are part of a higher essence and that anyone born
in the right place and of the right colour does not
need to prove his worth. His very existence makes
him superior. Because he belongs to his 'aristocracy
of the despicable' he has nothing to prove.[34] If, by
some misfortune, he discovers that other people have
their value too, his joy will be less savage because he
will have to take other opinions into account. The
feeling of belonging is much less exalting when his
guilt prevents him from laughing at other people,
crushing them or wiping them out.[35]

Collective amnesia is the rule, and negationism has
many advantages because it gives us a clear conscience,
rules to live by, and a delicious feeling of belonging
that means we never have to put ourselves in the
victim's place. This amputation of memory requires
us to burn books, silence witnesses and rewrite history.
Nothing could be easier for a fossilized order. The
negationist recipe is so effective that it has regularly
been used at every turning point in history. The Jewish
zealots of the first century tried to destroy all trace
of Jewish moderates. The Catholic Inquisition insisted
that there could be only one belief and spent 600 years

(from the thirteenth to the nineteenth century) using fire and sword to destroy all trace of those who did not think along the same lines. When the Nazis burned books in Berlin in 1933, they were deliberately constructing a memory. The same thing happened in the Colonels' Greece and Pinochet's Chile, and it happens in all social groups in which battles over the past reveal they are planning something they dare not admit. Collective memory is a conventional discourse, and it is in its interest to silence wounded souls and to valorize only those who justify it.

Society uses the individual memories implanted in our minds by the emotions of others to write its own history plays

Individual memories, for their part, are permeated by the environment. The sensory environment shapes certain parts of the brain, which become a template that sensitizes the individual to one kind of information. The human environment then gives certain events an emotional charge, and the individual then uses them to colour his or her recollections of the past.

If we left the argument at that, we would be forced to conclude that the individual is a receptacle in which the environment deposits few recollections. But our inner language and the stories we tell ourselves when we talk about ourselves and our histories allow us to acquire both a narrative identity and stable representations that make us feel that we are still the same, even though the environment changes and sometimes deals us some nasty blows.

A lot of our relational efforts go into making the two stories coincide. Each of them claims to be the truth. There is such a thing as a real world, and witnesses claim to have seen it with their own eyes. The real world also exists in the social narrative that urges them to describe what they have seen. But it is not the same real world.

It could be said that eye-witness accounts are institutional in nature, as children who have been isolated say that they find it difficult to remember events that occurred when they were living in isolation. We might also mention the institutional nature of eye-witness accounts,[36] and the institutional use that is made of memory.

When an important witness such as a deportee or war veteran takes part in a commemorative ceremony, we know nothing about his personality or history. But because he is there to act as a sign, he must display all the indices that remind us of the past: a coloured forage cap, a row of medals, striped pyjamas or a tattoo on the forearm are sufficient to suggest the appropriate story. The image he creates with his body and the signs he triggers just by being there evoke the tragedy: piles of bodies ... a smoking chimney ... the sadism of the Nazis who sniggered as they killed. The few survivors who took it upon themselves to bear witness in this way are scarcely aware of the fact that their sufferings have been transformed into a visual narrative, into a story without words that is similar to an advertisement. This thoughtless discourse is transformed into a stereotypical scenario which eventually ceases to have the emotional message it once had.

The survivor who is playing the role of the permanent representative of his own misfortunes is, in his inner world, on a very important mission. His act of witness allows him to transform his humiliation into a constructive message. He has a duty to remember so as to ensure that what happened to him never happens again. He is taking care of himself because, every time he describes the event, he transforms the emotions that are associated with it. His senseless sufferings acquire a meaning and become bearable because they give him a purpose in life. They are, however, completely out of step with the inner world of his listeners, or rather his spectators, because they have not had to undertake the work involved in a metamorphosis. When a former deportee is invited to address a gathering of young historians, he is there to recite a few terrible phrases, like a slogan that no one listens to any more.

In the 1950s young Bernard, who survived Auschwitz, was required to lay a wreath on his school's war memorial every year. In frozen silence he had to walk, carrying his wreath, between two lines of silent teachers and pupils. The memory of his sufferings and of the Holocaust had been transformed into a dusty ritual: a bored silence broken by the sound of his footsteps, his low bow. When the ceremonial chore was over, life began again. The faces lit up and the buzz of cheerful chatter began to evoke something else.

Is that what it was all about?

The constraints of 'why' and the fierce determination to bear witness immediately come up against the impossibility of communicating. It was his environment that forced the child to remain silent, and then criticized him for doing so. It was his environment that transformed his ordeal into a wordless story, a stereotypical piece of theatre, and then lost interest in it so as to make its life a little more comfortable, so as not to be embarrassed by its own guilt, and so as not to experience the feeling of indecency that is triggered by the misfortunes of others. And when, conversely, the obscenity of his sufferings triggers an emotional greed to hear more about them, the child is once more silenced.

A memory is not just a biological inscription of an event that is traced in the brain by the emotions of others. A memory has a history that has been inflicted on all wounded souls. When the memory is still fresh, trauma victims must turn it into a narrative that allows them to control their emotions and socialize their ordeal before they can begin to feel that they are now like other people.[37]

When the disaster strikes, the silence is stupefying. There is nothing to say. They have to keep quiet. But once the wounded have been more or less resocialized in a warehouse after the earthquake, in the Hôtel Lutétia after their deportation, or in some institution after they have been raped or assaulted, the noise of the chatter becomes deafening. Their listeners silence them almost immediately. Their carers sometimes force them to hold something back. It is almost as though they had to block off their memories. This goes some way to explaining the splitting and the way victims speak in roundabout ways when they insist on bearing witness at all cost.

The obligation to talk about their sufferings comes into conflict with the need to speak only of what is socially acceptable. This conflict produces staged memories. The victims were once silenced because their close relationship with their aggressors provoked the same feeling of disgust,[38] but their misfortunes are now being used to stage an official ideal. The very people who once maintained that those who survived the camps were suspect because, in their view, they must have collaborated with the enemy, now insist that a former deportee has to be present at all their political rallies.

As soon as the veterans' associations had frustrated the attempts to deny what had happened during the 1914–18 war, a conventional narrative was immediately elaborated. So much so that many *poilus* ended up saying only what their listeners wanted them to say: the 'pools of crimson blood' and the bayonet charges became deliciously horrifying clichés. It was impossible for them to bear witness to what really happened without breaking the spell and exposing themselves to criticism. The wounds that were cauterized by red-hot shrapnel in fact oozed pus rather than blood, and, when it did flow, the 'crimson blood' was immediately soaked up by the mud. And as for the bayonets, they were almost never used. But their narrative function is to idealize them as they tell the edifying tale of how a brave man of the people died a glorious death.

The witnesses themselves end up recounting the myths their ordeals have been turned into, rather than talking about the recollections that are inscribed in their memory. The prize-winning novels and the films whose images make us shed tears of admiration transform the fighters who lived in the mud with the cockroaches into shining heroes who have a responsibility to teach us about the courage and nobility of the common people. For it was the common people who saved the honour of France and not the officers, who disgraced themselves. Only one officer transcended the mediocrity of the decision-makers who were responsible for the slaughter of millions of men and the melancholy of a whole society: Marshal Pétain. But mythologizing his courage and honesty paved the way for his legitimate election as head of the Vichy government twenty years later on 11 July 1940, and then for his active involvement in another slaughter that a new negationism would in its turn attempt to normalize.

The need for the aesthetic is so great that an eye-witness account can break up the group by killing the myth

The need for the aesthetic is so great that it blurs reality. And yet objective accounts, when we have access to them, do have a greater emotional effect than myths. On the other hand, they desocialize us and break up the group because they kill myths. A witness who wishes to preserve his ties with the group therefore has to surrender to the myth. When he expresses what he remembers, he finds that he is on his own and is often a target for aggression. Descriptions of filthy wounds covered in mud, of interminable games of cards that helped to pass the time, of the emotional indifference of numbed men who accepted they would die an absurd death as they went to the latrines make listeners experience a silent disgust and encourage them to forget so as not to despise the victim-witness too much. In contrast, someone with the gift of the gab can find the words to transform the grim nausea of a stupid death into a glorious epic that is meaningful only within the context of the narrative. We adore false witnesses because they make us feel good by making the reality they transfigure bearable. If we wish to coexist and love one another, we have to surrender to the myth, not the truth. Woe betide anyone who tells the truth: he will be marginalized.

When little Bernard described the reality of how he was sentenced to death when he was imprisoned and deported, and described how the German soldiers, who were accompanied by French civilians wearing trilbies and dark glasses, came to arrest a six-year-old child one night, no one believed him, because that real event seemed so improbable at the time. And when he told the story of how he escaped, the adults burst out laughing because it sounded so incredible. One day a man who was decent enough, and probably a local worthy, said to him, 'Here, there's a few pennies to buy some sweets. You're good at making up stories.' It took just a few words to silence little Bernard for the next fifty years. We can only say what our culture wants to hear. But the wounded soul's compulsion to bear witness is so great that it becomes a form of torture. If he does not bear witness, he will become a traitor. But he can speak only if he conforms to the expressive criteria that are laid down by his culture.

The concerns of the present demand certain eye-witness accounts and silence others, rather as though our collective identity, or the cultural 'we' that exists only as a representation, needed a certain narrative about the past in order to bring its future plans to fruition.

After the liberation of France, the privileged witnesses were those who had been active in the resistance. Thanks to 200,000 people (out of a population of 40 million), every French citizen could enhance his or her own image and get over the defeat of 1940 and the humiliations of the occupation. Every narrative and every novel had to suggest that every French man and woman had been in the resistance, even when it was by no means obvious that they had. On seeing René Clair and Noël-Noël's film *Le Père tranquille* (1946), everyone thought that this family man lived in fear throughout the war. Don't be fooled, cinema-goers, his apparent submissiveness allowed him to do more for the resistance (like all of us, perhaps?). In the incredible cultural euphoria of the post-war years, the real world was desolate but the imaginary world was marvellous. The film was part of that imaginary world, as were all the novels and all the true eye-witness accounts produced by a culture that wanted nothing but wonderful stories about heroes.

When, in this context, Primo Levi, Robert Antelme,

David Rousset and many others tried to bear witness to the countless horrors they had had to endure, their culture denied them the right to speak.[39] In the 1980s, in contrast, people wanted to understand what had happened. There was no longer any pressing need to rebuild France's cities and families. It had become possible to look back and to try to understand the past. And in this very different context, the eye-witness accounts became meaningful.

In the 1950s, France had to turn a blind eye to the Vichy government's involvement in the cold violence of the first great administrative slaughter in history. A sub-prefect's signature that sentenced 1,990 adults and 263 children to death by administrative decree did not make much sense. When a few survivors said 'I was there', no one heard them. Indeed, those who had succeeded in socializing themselves attempted to silence them by explaining to them in learned terms that what they had seen never happened because it did not correspond to what they should have seen. The function of the psychosocial deafness of the decision-makers of the day was to preserve national unity and to sustain the enthusiasm for the rebuilding of France by silencing the witnesses. The problem raised in 1945 was understood only in 1981, by which time the social context had given this 'bureaucratic murder' a new meaning.[40]

But who was capable of understanding that, in the

social context of 1998, events no longer had the same meaning as in archives dating from between 1942 and 1944? When the documents that ordered the blankets, the coffee and the clean trucks were rediscovered, the former sub-prefect used them as an argument to prove that his actions had been humanitarian. Who was there to remember that a single blanket was used to keep together the children who shared it, because that made it easier to lock them in the trucks when the time came? The coffee was only distributed at night. It was compulsory, and that made it possible to beat people with rifle butts until they formed up in lines. That made it easier to take the roll call. As for the trucks, they were not used to transport the luggage, as the civil servant claimed.[41] They were sealed to ensure that none of the children escaped.

It was all true and the paperwork was all in order. According to the archives, there were blankets, coffee and trucks. But the meaning of those objects was quite different from what the archives said it was. In the reality of the war, they made it easier to kill, but in the story told in 1998 they became humanitarian aid. Their meaning is not inscribed in the archive, and it was in a different context, and a different climate, that hindsight changed the meaning of the facts.

Eye-witness accounts are always biased. It is because you have been sensitized to it by your past and your environment that you describe an event. The reason you are telling someone about it today is that you want your story to justify yourself, to take away your shame, or to influence society's version of it in order to change some collective representation. When Primo Levi learned that his book was about to be translated into German, he said, 'I feel myself being invaded by a new and violent emotion, the feeling of having won a battle ... It was really written for them, for the Germans, it was pointed at them like a gun.'[42]

The expression is eloquent. We can ask ourselves who the story of our memories is being aimed at. We cannot ask the same question about our memories themselves. We need them to construct our narrative identity. The things we have forgotten help us to make our autobiographical story more coherent, and ensure that we neither suffer too much nor fuel our own hatred. If we harbour life, we have to tell our stories. But if we harbour hatred, the story of our memories will become a weapon.

The need for coherent social narratives is so great that even the most generous institutions silence victims whose stories must not be told

No sooner had modern psychiatry emerged in the 1970s than a thesis written in 1981 revealed the negationism of certain psychiatrists.[43] I had heard vague talk of this. Certain administrators who had worked in psychiatric hospitals and a few nurses who were coming up to retirement age had told me about day-to-day life in the psychiatric hospitals during the war. But in that world, everyone was mad, not just the patients. Kind-hearted souls rubbed shoulders with a few monstrous nurses, and incredibly ignorant doctors worked alongside those who were on the point of discovering a new clinical and therapeutic approach.

In the cultural context of the psychiatric hospitals of the 1940s, there was a lot of talk about the struggle for existence, the survival of the fittest and, therefore, the elimination of the weakest. With 120,000 mental patients crowded together, the food shortages, the absence of care and the stated intention of eliminating those who were polluting the race,[44] it became easier to take the insidious decisions that caused the normal mortality rate in these strange hospitals to rise from 6.88 per cent in 1938 to 26.48 per cent in 1941. It was at this point that the first famine oedemas were described. But the 40,000 patients who died left no traces behind them and wrote no stories. The horrors they did recount when they were able to bear witness were regarded as terrible delusions, but it was French society that had gone mad. These patients died in silence, which is what was expected of them after the war, when there was a desire to rebuild the nation without settling accounts with the past.

Thanks to the way knowledge of this was obliterated, it was possible to reopen the psychiatric hospitals, to organize new competitive examinations, and to become a psychiatrist, a nurse or a manager without a care in the world. Denying what had happened helped to protect the decision-makers, who were now reluctant to uncover shameful secrets and who relativized the tragedy by implementing a revisionist strategy. They quibbled over the number of deaths, argued that 'normal people' went hungry too, and explained that many patients went to live with their families for the duration of the war. All of which is true.

The spontaneous way in which the story of tragedies evolves encourages this kind of revisionism. The final act in plays about the memories of the wounded is their normalization. No matter whether we are dealing with the subjective theatre of the memory that is imprinted on us by the reactions of those around us, or the public theatre in which the mythical story is declaimed, the production always goes back to humdrum horrors when the spotlights are turned off.

'Yes, but . . . It's not that serious . . . You can get over incest . . . We know the Germans were wicked . . . I can no longer stand school textbooks that talk about colonialism.' These are comments we habitually hear from people who indulge in a muted day-to-day revisionism because it makes them feel more at ease with themselves.

And of course everyone colludes with them. Victims like Charlotte Delbo would really like 'to step out of history/to enter life',[45] and so too would those who make such an effort not to listen to details that might disturb their afternoon nap. This protective denial is the source of the disorders that distort the relationship between the wounded and those who have a duty to care for them. The American troops who liberated the camps neither smiled at the living dead nor said a word to them as they watched themselves being watched with disgust. Practically all young incest victims make a cry for help. But we silence them by telling them that it is a fantasy, or that they must have led their fathers on. The children who survived the Holocaust were asked to provide death certificates for parents who had disappeared, just as we now ask Rwandan children to supply proof that the massacres they claim to have seen really happened. The children who survived are expected to pay contributions for so many years before they get their pensions; we make them travel, at great expense, to be given pullovers they cannot wear but which have been donated by some distant charity. We organize highbrow debates to determine whether or not the emaciated little survivors will be corrupted by the luxury hotels that were requisitioned to house them. Practically all the victims eventually use splitting mechanisms to try to adapt to this daily absurdity. The story they address to the 'normal' people who cannot understand them has nothing in common with the quasi-secret discourse they address to other victims who belong to the same world of horror.

The fact that their memories are socialized in two senses has a curious effect. A wounded individual who feels compelled to bear witness cannot say anything because society silences him. But society also requires him to remember so that the group's myth can feed on the story of his sufferings. The former deportee who stands in uniform at the foot of the memorial is acting out this obligation to remember. The same obligation to remember calls into the witness box the child who has been raped, and forces her to describe in public her sexual humiliations to an audience of professionals who have a vested interest in her story. And the same obligation allows a reformed communist like Paul Rassinier to become the founding father of French revisionism by saying that he did not suffer during his deportation, and that he never saw any chimneys. More importantly, it lies at the source of the false-memory syndrome.

When we began to work on the problem of incest in the 1970s, people reacted in two very different ways. The most common reaction was denial, as when the doctor said to his fiancée, 'You must have fantasized it.' Collective denial explains why a primary schoolteacher had to leave the village where he taught because he had denounced an incestuous father: the neighbours sprang to the man's defence. It also explains why a journalist who had asked me some strange questions suddenly declared: 'I don't believe you. The children would say "no".'

The joys of false memory

At one extreme, we have denial; at the opposite, we find a dubious enthusiasm for these fascinating victims. A Recovered Memory Movement was started in the United States in 1980. 'Psychotherapists' began to recover what they said were previously repressed traumatic memories. This gave rise to a series of highly publicized trials in which large numbers of fathers were grilled and condemned in public, until the 'victims' themselves admitted that they had never been sexually assaulted and began to wonder, somewhat late in the day, where their terrible 'repressed memories' came from.

The psychologist Elizabeth Loftus has always been dubious about the irremediable nature of the sexual traumas that supposedly give rise to all kinds of neuroses. She herself was raped as a girl but was able to initiate a resilience process that allowed her to become fulfilled as an adult woman. Not surprisingly, the psychology of memory is her special subject of interest.

The pseudo-psychoanalytic argument goes as follows:

'The reason you are having problems now is that you were raped as a girl and that repression prevented you from recovering the memory of the assault. All you have to do to get back to normal is to verbalize your memories.' The practice enjoyed spectacular success in the United States, and is now becoming more common in France. The explanation is obvious: 'memory surprises us again and again with its gee-whiz gullibility'.[46]

Suggestibility and hypnosis have acquired such a bad name that we underestimate the psychology of influence. Some modern authors, such as Tobie Nathan, Daniel Bougnoux and Jean Léon Beauvois, have dusted down the concept of influence in various disciplines, and have shown how people's memories can be manipulated. They have demonstrated that false memories can be implanted in the mind, and can even trigger sincere accounts of events that occurred only in the mind of the experimenter.[47] Influence can modify an autobiographical narrative and alter a self-image. An individual's feeling of shame can be removed by altering the image she has of herself. This is what happens in psychotherapeutic processes, but a mother's influence on her child, a father's influence on his family or a cultural group's influence on its members has the same effect. The process of influence allows us to coexist because we share the same myth. The mere fact of experiencing a shared emotion, of worshipping the same representation and observing the same rituals together, gives us a delicious feeling of belonging. But we have to be careful. Lies are not the enemy of truth, but myths are. We distrust lies and try to repress them, but we love myths and ask for nothing better than to surrender to them. It is not persuasion that leads to submission; it is the behavioural *mise en scène* that structures emotions and gives them currency.[48]

Given that we now know that memory is bound up with our emotions, the experimental findings suggest that relationships are easier to remember than events. We therefore become imprinted with the bonds we establish with people who have an emotional impact on us. Moments of love and terrifying events therefore become the cornerstones of the biographical edifice. We give those who make an emotional impact on us the power to leave their mark. In the words of singer-songwriter Georges Brassens, 'Never in your life will you forget the first girl you held in your arms.' And the memory of that delicious moment will become a chronological marker in your life story. A cultural event that gets a lot of media coverage can have the same effect. I was at my mother-in-law's on the day that President Kennedy was shot. Were it not for that truly astonishing event, I would have completely forgotten about that enjoyable visit.

But there is worse: hate is an emotion too. Indeed, we allow those we hate to shape our memories and play a part in shaping our identity just as much as those

we love. In his *Vipère au poing*, the novelist Hervé
Bazin describes how he organized the construction of
his identity around Folcoche – the mother he hated.
The memories of children who have been abused are
like a film that they project for themselves in the inner
world of their recollections whenever some minor incident triggers them: 'As soon as I raise my hand to my
children it reminds me of my mother, and that makes
me so sad that I stop.' To the end of her days, the
beautiful, poignant Barbara regretted the fact that the
father who, one night in Tarbes, plunged her into a
world of horror, died without ever saying the words
of repentance that would have allowed the singer to
forgive him and to stop hating him. 'Before he died,
he wanted / to warm himself in my smile / but he
died that same night / without saying "Goodbye",
without saying "I love you".'[49] A myth is a powerful
social representation, so powerful that hate can cause
it to imbue every memory.

In the United States certain representations of abuse
became so contagious that they spread like wildfire. The
'victims' joined Survivors of Incest Anonymous, studied
The Courage to Heal,[50] wrote to one another, read the
same books. Some women felt slightly embarrassed, but
the psychotherapists' theoretical explanations enabled
them to overcome their doubts with just a few words.
There was a real improvement in their mental health,
and these lonely women were revitalized and began to

travel, read and talk again. They were living in the same world as other victims who could commune because they had all been hurt in the same way. They could at last explain why their lives had been so painful ever since they were girls. Once they knew what caused the pain, they could operate.

Sexual abuse was becoming profitable. It is easier to live in a group, and there is a reason you are in such pain. It is easier to get a divorce, and a little therapeutic compensation. Woe betide anyone who has any doubts; she will be expelled from the group. When a victim tells the story her social group expects her to tell, it worships her: 'You've suffered so much; tell us what happened. But you only have the right to tell us what we want to hear.' When a victim makes the mistake of describing how she survived and recovered from her ordeal, she is immediately accused of being in denial or of colluding with her aggressor because she has spoiled the pleasure of surrendering to the myth.

The mystery consists of asking ourselves why people are so often stopped from bearing witness, and why they are sometimes the focus of attention. We should not be saying, 'You've been hurt, so you're finished.' We should really be asking, 'What are you going to do with your wounds? Are you going to give in and become a professional victim, so as to give those who want to help you a clear conscience? Are you going to get your revenge by going public about what happened to you, so as to make your aggressors or the people who refused to help you feel guilty? Are you going to use your tragedy to promote an ideology that will make it an issue in a power struggle? Are you going to suffer in silence and wear your smile as a mask? Or are you going to strengthen the healthy part of yourself so as to heal your wounds and become human after all?'

The conspiracy of silence that everyone colludes in is certainly the least painful strategy. The wounded soul grits her teeth, but if she groans, protests or just talks about her pain, the ordinary listener is embarrassed, talks about obscenity and accuses the trauma victim of stripping off in public. But if the victim says nothing, she loses control over her inner language. Stories that have never been told and delicious or horrible phantasmagorias introduce turmoil into the world of men and women who remain motionless and silent.

If it were not for our memories of how we were hurt, we would be neither happy nor unhappy: we would be forced to live in the present

If we wish to adopt the strategy of silence, the best way to ensure that no one tells stories or talks about what they remember is to live for the moment without bothering about the future or dwelling on the past. It is our ability to represent time that makes us unhappy. Live in the present, and all will be well.

There are naturalistic medical experiments that allow us to find out if living for the moment and forgetting about how we were hurt really does lead to happiness. Road accidents cause thousands of brain injuries every year, and we therefore have more than enough clinical data to discuss. The gap in the victim's memory means that he cannot remember the accident or what happened immediately before it. But if the gap is wider, and lasts for a period of months or even years, then all the biographical details of what happened before the accident may be erased. This is defined as retrograde amnesia. Anteretrograde amnesia, which is very common in the elderly, is defined by the inability to recall recent events as time passes. The individual concerned can often recall distant biographical events with astonishing clarity. Whilst he can no longer remember what happened yesterday, he can accurately recall the names of the children he went to school with between the ages of six and eight, the words spoken by a teacher sixty years earlier, and all the other details that stay with a child.

Retrograde amnesia wipes out the patient's pre-traumatic biography, but anteretrograde amnesia means that *only* his pre-traumatic biography is inscribed in his memory. From our point of view, the interesting thing about these conditions is that they allow us to observe how stories, verbal behaviours and the feeling of selfhood vary in accordance with these different forms of memory.

A man who was involved in a road accident is suffering from retrograde amnesia. When he goes back to the golf course where he worked as a greenkeeper for five years, he loses his way and says that he does not know where he is, but has a strange feeling: something is uncannily familiar.[51] His perception of his place of work is feeding into a representation that he no longer recognizes. In this environment, his sense of self becomes distorted. Because he no longer has a past, he is living in a world that is always new.

The feelings triggered by this perception of a world that has no past find expression in verbal behaviours that we can learn to read. His eyes do not focus on anything in particular. He frowns and stands still in bewilderment. It takes him a long time to answer questions, and his speech is flat and devoid of verbal melody. His verbal behaviour provides a clue as to how he feels about himself: when the retrograde amnesia begins to fade and when the subject rediscovers his past, his speech becomes fluent, confident, lively and musical. When his past was missing, every aspect of his verbal behaviour was an expression of the confusion he felt. As soon as he began to remember his history, his wounded soul was able to express a range of emotions.

When they recover their memories, amnesiac patients tell us that their thoughts were disorganized and that their perception of the world did not make sense. The greenkeeper could see the golfers perfectly well, but the way they were behaving looked absurd; their actions were appropriate in that environment but they were meaningless to him. Our perception of the real world has to include the dimension of time. It is because we can compare them with earlier circumstances that events make sense.

If we wish to understand how a film ends, we have to remember how it began. We understand that our hero is proud to have become a ticket collector at the Porte des Lilas metro station because we recall that he escaped from the prison hulks in Toulon. Conversely, we can understand that he is ashamed of being a ticket collector because we remember that he was once on the board of a water company. Whether or not we assume that the ticket collector feels proud or ashamed depends on our own ability to integrate time, and to evoke the past in order to make sense of the present. We can only put ourselves in someone else's place or empathize with them if we can understand what their situation means to them and how they got into it.

The neurological substrate of this memory is organized in the brain circuits that associate the prefrontal lobe, which controls our ability to look into the future, with the limbic brain, which controls our emotions and memory. The loss of blood resulting from a brain injury damages that zone. Although their origins are different, inadequate parenting or even a political decision that results in sensory deprivation can, in such cases, interfere with the workings of this part of the brain, and make it organically impossible to make sense of what we perceive. A damaged family or social environment makes it impossible for us to tell our stories, and making sense of things then becomes a cultural impossibility.

Lobotomies and aphasia illustrate this organic inability to tell stories. But it is the shame and secrecy that create the cultural handicap.

When a road accident causes a minor haemorrhage in the prefrontal lobes, the blood dilacerates the neurological connections, and sometimes performs a perfect lobotomy. We have known for more than a century that the frontal personality of the victim undergoes astonishing changes in a fraction of a second: the victim loses all sense of the future and has no image of how the world is changing. Phinéas Gage, who was the first person known to have been lobotomized, was a disciplined and meticulous worker until the day an iron bar went through his eye and severed both frontal lobes.[52] From that moment onwards he was euphoric because he no longer had any worries about the future. But at the same time he became unstable because, being incapable of planning ahead, he no longer responded to the stimuli of the present.

This neurological inability to imagine the future results in radical changes in verbal behaviour and sentence structuring.[53] Whereas people who are chatty like meeting other people socially because it allows them to feel some emotion and to share a few representations, someone who has been lobotomized makes no effort to meet others because he or she has no sense that there is a future. When he is spoken to, he responds appropriately, but in sentences that are short, taciturn and monosyllabic. There are no commas or relative conjunctions. In order to punctuate a sentence that requires us to take a breath or use a relative pronoun, we have to know in advance what we are going to say. Because he has no sense of time, someone who has been lobotomized does not require that grammar. Short answers are all he needs.

The context, or rather the co-text, of what he says is astonishingly devoid of gestures and facial expressions.[54] Because he has no intention of influencing others, he does not need to use facial expressions or emphatic gestures to make his point. His lack of empathy makes him quite indifferent to social judgements. That is why he sometimes urinates in public. He does not have a problem with his bladder and his behaviour is not antisocial. He is simply responding to his needs of the moment because he cannot look ahead, and has no idea of the emotions he might trigger a second later in the minds of others. He is simply responding to the immediate stimulus of a full bladder.

He does not move because he has no intention of doing anything, but he is not apathetic and responds vigorously when he is jostled. If he is in a noisy, hectic environment, he will run in all directions, shouting 'I'm in a hurry ... I'm in a hurry!' When the environment calms down, so does he: he sits down and lapses back into silence. When no one is looking at him, he simply lives in the present.

He no longer experiences the emotional effort that goes into speaking. When we cannot find the word we need, we feel an unpleasant tension: 'the thing that goes over the water ... across a river'. Because the word escapes us, we become tense and use words and gestures to express ourselves in roundabout ways. If we cannot find the appropriate circumlocution, we snap our fingers or make clicking noises with our tongues. And then we suddenly find the word we were looking for: 'A bridge!' Just being able to articulate the word calms us down. It is quite astonishing and almost magical: a word has an effect on the body. We can understand that if we accept the idea that our sentences and stories give others – and ourselves – a feeling of having a coherent identity, and therefore allow us to influence the world around us. Anyone who lives in neither the past nor the future is forced to live in the present. He can solve the problems that are raised by his perception of his context. So he does think. But his world of representations does not extend very far: he does not tell himself stories about the future, and his past has no history. He needs no representations to modify others' representations, and he therefore has no need for stories.

When someone who has been lobotomized cannot find the word he wants, he stops speaking, does not move, shows no sign of being annoyed, and does not try to find another word. If we read him *Little Red Riding Hood*, he is familiar with the story because he has no memory troubles. If we deliberately introduce some absurdity into the story, he notices it immediately because he is no fool. But if we ask him to go on with the story, which he knows by heart, he will stop after one or two sentences.

This natural experiment, which damages the neurological substrate that allows us to imagine the future, makes it impossible to tell stories. And that allows us to understand that our stories about the past are future-oriented, and that when we search our memories, we are looking for a few details that we can turn into a story.

The intentionality of memory is largely directed at both other people and ourselves. It is a representation, a *mise en scène* of words and images that have been imprinted on us by other people. We then tell others our story in order to modify their representations to suit our own purposes.

When we are liberated from others, we become prisoners of the present. Because we have been imprinted by other people, we can influence them by using words which, because they move them, imprint us in our turn. Any story is largely a co-production.

A combination of the butterfly effect of speech and narrative identity obliges us to speak

A sort of 'thought transmission' occurs when words and the inner worlds of the people who are speaking fuse. In this airy world where words represent inner images, speech has a 'butterfly effect': the very fact of getting ready to speak is a relief to our sense-perception of our own bodies. I am not suggesting that we have to contrast speech with biology, as our misleading academic division of labour teaches us to do; I am suggesting that speech is to the body what the butterfly is to the caterpillar. The butterfly and the caterpillar live in different worlds; one floats through the air, and the other clings to leaves. But they do exist in a continuum. The butterfly would not exist if it had never been a caterpillar. It is the astonishing process of metamorphosis that makes the transition from larva to imago possible. Similarly, our children live in a world of preverbal understanding before they can talk and then, over a period of twenty months, they slowly prepare to undergo the metamorphosis of speech.[55] Young children understand words long before they have mastered them.[56] As soon as they begin to use words, the way they use their bodies undergoes a metamorphosis.

When we become tense because we cannot find the word we are looking for, we try to calm ourselves down by using other words instead, or express ourselves in roundabout ways by using gestures to point to or illustrate what we mean. The fact that we use more self-centred gestures, become slightly annoyed with ourselves, and use facial expressions, vocalizations and postures that externalize our inner irritation is a behavioural index of how uncomfortable we feel. When we cannot find the words we are looking for, we mistreat our emotions and we use archaic means of expression to try to calm down.

Clinical neurology describes two situations in which the subject loses the power of speech for a few hours. As soon as the subject recovers it, he is astonished to find that he feels as light as a butterfly, whereas he felt as heavy as lead just a few hours before.

A fifty-eight-year-old lady who often suffered migraines was doing her shopping in a supermarket. She needed to buy oil and sugar, but suddenly had the feeling that her whole body had become strangely heavy. In her inner world, she could hear the signifier 'oiloiloiloil', but the sound no longer referred to the object, 'a bottle of oil'. She said to herself, or realized, 'I've got another migraine, I should take some aspirin', but could not say the words. She thought of asking the check-out assistant where the cafeteria was, but to her astonishment she heard herself saying: 'Wherecan, where can, can . . . drink.' She understood that the assistant was telling her to go in that direction, but her words were just strange sounds. When, a few minutes later, the visual migraine began, the woman felt that her exhausted body was racked with pain, but she was relieved to find that she could talk once more.

Monsieur M was writing something when his pen slowed down for some strange reason, rather as though he had lost control of his hand, which suddenly felt heavy. He thought of telephoning his wife but could not dial the number. So he dragged himself into his seventeen-year-old son's room to ask him to phone his mother, but all he could say was 'Telphonema'. He realized that he must be creating a strange impression in his son's mental world because he could not pronounce the words properly. He tried to reassure him by patting him on the back and saying 'telphonema'. Which quite naturally made the adolescent feel even more worried.

A few hours later, Monsieur M recovered the power of speech and explained how he had felt in the strange mental world he had been living in during his aphasic episode. Although he lost the ability to use words, he had still been capable of organizing visual representations. It was rather like being in a silent film. He had gone back to living in an inner world that was semanticized by images.

Being unable to speak does not prevent us from empathizing, whereas someone who has had a lobotomy is perfectly capable of speech but could not care less about the impression his image makes on the mind of other people. It is therefore not the use of linguistic or physical signs that allows us to inhabit someone else's world; it is our neurological ability to perceive time and to represent it in the form of verbal or visual narratives. On the other hand, the ability to speak does influence the way we experience our own bodies.

When one of my psychoanalyst friends lost the power of speech for a few hours after suffering a cerebral embolism, he suddenly realized that the primary function of speech is to weave emotional bonds: 'the speaking being becomes attached to the first speaking being who comes along'.[57] Within the space of just a few seconds, he realized to his astonishment that, although he was unable to speak, he had been resensitized to the stimuli that came from his environment. He understood that his doctors were talking about him but were no longer talking to him. Indeed, when the consultant sat on the edge of his bed to say a few words to him, he was not wasting his time because, even though the patient could not understand what he was saying, he did understand that the consultant was sitting beside him and speaking to him. The patient was deeply moved by the change of posture, which communicated the doctor's emotional intentions. When the consultant left, the patient lay completely still; he was clinging to the marks the doctor had left on the sheets when he crumpled them. Although he had lost the power of speech, the patient could perceive tiny sensory indices, and was overwhelmed by them. He could not tear himself away from them.

The very fact that we can speak gives a feeling of selfhood with a spatial and temporal extension. The moment the blood begins to circulate in the temporal zone that controls language, the patient recovers the power of speech. The mere fact of being able to use words to imagine a world with a spatial and temporal extension modifies our sense of selfhood so much that we begin to feel light. We know that impression is not due to the cessation of the paralysis, for elderly people who are gradually losing access to verbal language describe the same feeling. What is more, adults who cannot find the words they are looking for are not paralysed, but they do feel that their bodies are heavy and tense: 'My whole body was physically straining to find the words ... It's heavy ... the lack ... growing anxiety.'[58]

All the aphasics who were interviewed after they had recovered the power of speech used metaphors of weight and enclosure: 'A thought was ready. I said to myself: "So it's true, I can't speak any more" ... The telephone rang, I picked it up to reply but, to my great surprise, the words would not come ... It was like being walled up.'[59]

The loss of speech modifies our representation of the world. When a patient can no longer evoke other spaces, she becomes contextual. The feeling of self-hood becomes proximal and is defined by the sensory environment. 'Without words, my body reverted to being meat.'[60] The aphasic psychoanalyst was also astonished at how powerful his dreams became during sleep in the the few hours after he lost the ability to speak. As he was no longer living in the world of verbal representations, his world was defined by sensorial stimuli by day, and, at night, by the impressions that had been traced on his memory and then reactivated when his dreams stimulated his brain.

The less we speak, the more we feel the weight of the context. But as soon as we begin to speak, we feel what our words represent. We have to choose: we can either surrender to the impressions implanted in us by our environment, or surrender to the feelings triggered by our representations.

When the power of speech returns, the counter-experiment begins. Former aphasics experience an astonishingly 'light, spacy' feeling of selfhood. Their words spin metaphors: 'clouds . . . travelling through space . . . seven-league boots . . . I climb on to a bird's back, its wings flap, I close my eyes. Oh, the little spots have gone.'[61]

The 'butterfly effect of speech' really does mean something. The organic inability to produce words makes us feel leaden but we also experience emotional difficulties when we try to talk to those close to us.

As for the social discourse that prevents wounded souls from bearing witness in order to keep official declarations consistent, it too gives a feeling of mental leadenness and blocks self-expression. Wounded souls adapt to the obligation to remain silent by using splitting mechanisms: because one part of the personality has been amputated, the undamaged part can go on expressing itself in socially acceptable ways.

'When I was a child, I told the truth . . . and I got, shall we say, slaps in return.'[62] Even though René Char was told to keep quiet, he still found ways to express himself. The splitting mechanisms he was forced to use created two different mental worlds inside his mind: the outer world gave a pretty, valorized self-image, but his inner world created a darker and more painful self-image. The two spaces were not cut off or separated from one another; if they had been, the poet would have been dissociated and incoherent. They established a strange mode of communication organized around silence.

The external image adapts to family emotions, institutional constraints and social myths, whilst the internal image is destined to become stereotypical.

A secret is a mental working drawing – that is why it has such great emotional power; thoughts are physically transmitted in para-speech

The tiny watercolours painted by Delacroix during his trip to Morocco consist of a couple of lines drawn in pencil and a few splashes of colour. Too much detail would have diminished their evocative power by distracting the viewer's attention. By reducing them to essentials and getting rid of all interference, he heightened the impression of bright colours and exoticism. The same thing happens in symbol formation; a couple of gestures, a few sounds or a single image can do more to evoke an absent object than its actual presence. Wounded souls who are not allowed to talk about the details and the emotions triggered by the assault they suffered glimpse a scenario of the aggression every night. Despite what people say, they do not, however, relive it. When they think about it, they do not feel what they felt at the moment of impact. The wounded soul is no longer subjected to the immediate constraints of the real world, and that is all it takes to make an outline version of their tragedy reappear on their inner stage. He sees the images again and hears the words again, but they now have the simplicity that comes from the power of clarity. Its stylization increases the power of the revised trauma.[63] The more stylized the memory, the greater its power.

Anyone who is keeping a secret is in the same position. For the benefit of the outside world, he projects an image which is often based on the quiet morbidity he associates with a sort of internal crypt where a stylized horror films is screened every night.[64] When our private memories cannot be articulated with what the public remembers, there are whole episodes in our history that cannot be put into words. The sense of having a stable and coherent identity that comes from being able to tell one's own story is split into a clear part that can be valued by society, and a dark, shameful part we cannot admit to. The butterfly effect of the words we are holding back then begins to fly in a strange way: the butterfly flits around and then suddenly begins to fly in circles. Similarly, wounded souls chat away quite happily and then suddenly begin to stammer.

This metaphor illustrates the idea that all secrets reveal something. We can describe secretive behaviour in the terms suggested by the word's etymology: 'secret' derives from the same root as 'secrete', to excrete something shameful, to sieve, to filter what we can say so as to hold back what we cannot reveal. All the speakers who, over thousands of years, shaped the word's meaning were already thinking about the protective function of secrets. Silence does more to protect the soul of a child than the explanations that are meant to protect her. All she has to do is keep quiet and barricade herself in. And besides, children feel very safe and strong when they realize that they can, if they wish, keep a secret. But when a wounded past cannot be talked about because violent emotions prevent us from telling our story, we hear the halting words, the trembling voice, the change of subject or the unexpected silence that betrays the trouble caused by the obligation to remain silent. The gaps in our speech, the behavioural stammer that suddenly punctuates an over-articulate verbal sequence, provide clues to the mystery and show us where the secret lies. All secrets are open secrets. Things that cannot be talked about are filtered through para-speech.

Victims are indecent. They ruin our dinner parties. So they keep quiet. But when they say nothing at all, their silent presence does even more to ruin our dinner parties. Because they cannot say everything, they use para-speech. And their secrets produce a strange language.

When this happens, a mystery is being revealed. Banalities disappear when our behaviour underlines them and turns them into enigmas. 'It's funny. Whenever the word "incest" is mentioned on the TV, my mother gets edgy and leaves the room.' The young woman who told me this does not know that I know her mother. Her mother confided in me that she did indeed have an incestuous relationship with her brother, who was seriously ill. 'I will never say anything about it,' she told me. 'It would kill my mother.' She never said anything, but she did use para-speech. Like some strange attractor, her unusual behaviour showed where the mystery lay.

Objects can become enigmatic too. When someone with a secret uses them, she alone knows what they mean. The meaning she gives them modifies the emotions of those around her; they sense that something has changed but do not really understand what that something is. That is why a photo album could cause a family row. And why a mouldy old sofa became a symbol of the struggle against anti-Semitism.

When Monsieur and Madame M got married, they knew perfectly well that they could never have sexual relations. But they wanted so much to have a child that they decided to adopt a baby 'as soon as its mother gave birth', and swore never to talk about it. When she was about eight, the girl became hell to live with. Her fits of anger and reproachfulness were always triggered by the same scenario: every time she took out the photo album to ask the ritual questions that inscribe a child in a line of descent – 'Who's that?' 'That's cousin Berthe.' 'Who's that?' 'That's Grandad Gaston' – her parents, who felt uncomfortable and wanted to keep the secret, answered her questions so badly that the girl became agitated. When, a few years later, she wanted to provoke her parents, all she had to do was take out the album; the stylized action was all it took to trigger the usual scenario. Simply touching the album and glancing at her mother was enough to start a row. In the end, everyone came to agree that the album had evil powers. And it did have evil powers, because it pointed to her parents' secret and their shame. The album, which everyone could see, materialized the story that had been hidden away. It pointed to something obscure: the mystery surrounding the girl's origins that made the family so anxious. Had the relationship been less fraught, the same object would have taken on a different meaning. It would still have been magical, but it would have been a source of delight. When words are silenced, objects become a language.

That is how Madame D got her sofa to talk. Throughout her childhood, she had never succeeded in exchanging two kinds words with her mother, a strict, curt woman who was active in an anti-Semitic cult. Fortunately, her grandmother was much kinder, and often invited her to share a cup of hot chocolate as they sat chatting on an old sofa. When she was twenty, by which time she had become a social worker, she met a law student. She found him interesting, but there was nothing more to it than that. But when the budding lawyer asked her to marry him and told her he was Jewish, she accepted on the spot 'to annoy my mother', who, naturally enough, did not attend the ceremony. Feeling sorry for her, her grandmother said she would come, but died two days before the wedding. When the time came to divide up her grandmother's possessions, the young woman asked for the old sofa, and, of course, no one objected. Thirty years later, her husband, who is now a wealthy lawyer, wonders why his wife still hangs on to a mouldy sofa when they have such beautiful furniture. No one else in the family knows, but for her the sofa 'means' that her mother is excluded from her emotional circle. The sofa winks at her to tell her that her grandmother is still alive.[65]

Perhaps there are no families without secrets. Our homes are our official discourse, but they may be full of objects that can talk. They may be hiding a few trinkets that whisper stories that our families do not want to hear. Objects that show off attract less attention than objects that whisper.

Gisèle was fifteen when she joined the resistance in

Bordeaux. She had been told not to look at the notices the Gestapo put up because, if she appeared to be showing an interest in them, she would be followed. She had been taught to use a revolver. No one suspected anything when the tall girl walked up to the local Gestapo commander in the village square until she shot him dead. Thirty hostages were executed the next day. Whenever Gisèle passed through the village after liberation, she thought to herself, 'That child is an orphan . . . because of me. That woman is living in poverty . . . because of me. That business went bankrupt . . . because of me.' She never stopped expiating her guilt through her self-punishing behaviour but she never talked about it. For fifty years, none of her children ever asked her about the significance of the strange bundle of oily rags she kept in an iron box in the middle of the bookshelf, in full view. It was her fifteen-year-old grandson who, having discovered that it contained a revolver, asked her why it was there. So his grandmother told him the object's story. She had placed it there as a sign, but no one had noticed it. When the war is over, you stop talking about it. There is no point in stirring up the past, is there? So she kept seeing the scene and punished herself in secret. She was really surprised by the relief she got from simply telling the boy her story. She felt that she had filled in a huge hole in her biography, that she had become whole and coherent, rather as though she had sewn together two parts of a personality that had been torn apart.

When we keep quiet about a secret, we make other things talk about it, but those around us often make sure that they hear nothing. Aïcha was frustrated because she knew almost nothing about her father. 'He does not exist in this house. I don't know where he was born. He never talks about himself.' And then she found a packet of photographs and an official family record book in the room where she had slept as a child. 'I'd had those things in my hand and held them, but I'd never looked at them. If my mother had been able to love me, I would have looked at the photos and asked questions about where I came from.'

When speaking is difficult, we express ourselves in para-speech, but the witnesses often shut their eyes and block their ears. They have everything they need to understand, apart from the desire to be involved. The artist Niki de Saint Phalle never really hid her 'darkest secret'.[66] The very pseudonym she chose was designed to give it away. What is hidden is meant to be understood. She is using para-speech to describe what, for her, was a summer in hell: 'The summer of the snakes, when my father – the aristocrat, the banker – put his penis in my mouth. I've survived death, and I needed to let the little girl inside me have her say at last' . . . fifty years later.[67]

The hidden secret is not always tragic, but it always

bears witness to something shameful or to the difficulty of accepting some part of oneself. Aurora was pretty, and knew all there was to know about Italian culture. She said that she had the complexion of a Sicilian, but her forename recalled the fact that she was born in the Aurès mountains of Algeria. She loathed the idea of being Algerian, unlike her parents, who were nostalgic for their homeland. Her name revealed something she wanted to hide, but also allowed her to reach a compromise. She could show her love for her family and at the same satisfy her desire to deny her origins, and therefore integrate into Western culture more easily. This common defence mechanism has one immediate advantage – 'I am adapting to a society that has been aggressive towards me' – but it also plants a time bomb and creates a false self: 'I am trying to be something I am not.'

Keeping a secret can damage a relationship;
disclosing a secret can change everything,
which some people find hard to bear

When a secret is kept, something else is let slip, and that something can damage both the individual and those close to him. But if it is disclosed, things have to be reworked, and those who are closest to him cannot always accept that.

The children of parents with secrets often behave strangely or negatively: they rarely ask questions. It is difficult to observe this restraint, as it is a non-behaviour. Not that that stops a reserved child from making an impression on those around them. Such restraint is therefore an observable behavioural typology that explains the characteristic relational ambience of every family.

It is possible that such children see in their parents a behavioural strangeness that makes them keep quiet. 'Dad is cheerful and hard-working, but he freezes when anyone talks about Armenia.' When children who are born of incestuous relationships fail to ask questions about their fathers, it is their silence that reveals the problem and their refusal to speak that raises questions. This 'cryptic behaviour'[68] is typical of the relational style of families with a secret in which both parents and children act strangely and pass on their strange behaviour from one generation to the next.

Monsieur Paul's little boy died in Auschwitz, where he was the victim of medical experiments. After the war, the wounded father tenderly brought up his other children, who, sensing that something inside their father's soul had died, never talked about their dead brother. During this period, the silence was complete. When Monsieur Paul became a grandfather, his love for his grandson knew no bounds and he adored looking after him. When he gave the boy an expensive teddy bear for this third birthday, the child unhesitatingly named it after the boy who had died. Monsieur Paul's behaviour clearly indicated that he was dumbfounded; his reaction moved the boy and implanted in his mind a feeling of strangeness that he attributed to his teddy bear. It was as though the child had said to himself: 'I really love my grandfather, and I am therefore very sensitive to all the signals he sends out. Everything he does makes an impression on me. But when he sees my teddy, he behaves strangely. So what is it about this teddy bear?' Thanks to a single emotion triggered by a behavioural event, Monsieur Paul's tragedy seeped into the bear. Thought transmission is not something that happens in the ether. On the contrary, it was the immense pain experienced in 1944 that imbued a teddy bear given to a child in 1974 with the feeling that something was not right, and it did so materially, sensually and physically. [69] 'A family secret can sometimes be hidden away in some everyday object . . . that commemorates a memory that cannot be talked about . . . the accidental destruction of such an object has a major impact on one or other of the descendants . . . and can trigger . . . emotional attitudes or behaviours whose meaning escapes them and forces them to behave like that without realizing it,' explains Serge Tisseron.[70]

Those who believe in family ghosts are held prisoner by a silent memory that circulates without a word being spoken and is transmitted in para-speech. Those who believe that there are such things as families without ghosts surrender to the immediate by amputating their past. Ghosts have enormous power because they live in para-speech and because, without realizing it, we put them into the objects we use in our everyday lives. Ghosts are prowlers who, long after the event has died, suddenly reappear because we carry them in the language we speak and the things we inherit. Ghosts do not transmit the trauma directly because those who come back from the grave make us relive a past history which, in a different context, takes on a different meaning and triggers different emotions. But they can transmit a turmoil or a feeling of discomfort which can damage our descendants. They can also bequeath a question or a mystery that encourages them to explore the archaeology or a poetics of knowledge: people who have almost died find something miraculous in the most banal aspects of life. Those who have almost lost a loved one have an acute sense of his or her presence because he or she was once present as a matter of routine. Children without families are obliged to become archaeologists.

Like all those who have inherited a ghost, the Armenians of the Diaspora 'are confronted with the twofold manifestation of the torturer's perversion: murder and its denial'.[71] One million people were killed with cold steel in the space of a week. 'Not only did I have to die,' says the ghost, 'I also have to tell you that I am not dead and that I am exaggerating.' When a child's memory is visited by a ghost who speaks like this, he has to identify with a lineage that has disintegrated. 'So what? My parents fled Armenia for trivial reasons at a time when there was nothing to worry about. And I'm supposed to identify with them and inscribe myself within the lineage of those cowards!'

'Your parents were exaggerating,' says the negationist. 'No more than 800,000 died, or perhaps just 500,000, and they died of cold or typhus. The army and the prisoners who had been deliberately released slaughtered no more than 100,000 Armenians; and there was a danger that your parents would take the side of the Russians.' A negationist who speaks like this is relativizing the crimes of the ancestors with whom he identifies. 'They were good people, and they didn't do much wrong. A minor crime, a mere detail in the 100,000-year history of the "Wise Man".' But when he normalizes their crimes, the negationist reveals that he identifies with the killers. When he polishes their image, he betrays his own intentions: he wants to continue their work.

Modern Armenians refuse to allow their lineage to disintegrate. 'They bear witness to the classic three-generation pattern: the first generation survived the massacre, made an effort to adapt ... the second profited from their efforts and the money they accumulated ... the third is ... looking for its roots.'[72]

The ghosts have declared war on each other. The negationists' ghosts use the same arguments, examples and turns of phrase as their murderous ancestors. But the grandchildren of the persecuted are looking for ghosts who can tell them about their roots.

When ghosts wage war on one another and try to kill each other, the representation of the trauma hurts their children even more

Whenever there are secrets, the atmosphere is always stormy. 'What's going on? Why does everything feel so strange? Is it because my father never says anything? Because my mother keeps her eyes lowered? Or because this is such a strange object? My parents are not like other people. They have experienced something exceptional, like supermen ... or subhumans.' We can easily go from one emotional extreme to the other, and our moods change in the twinkling of an eye. But on the whole, children whose parents were martyred are proud of the ordeals they survived; 69 per cent of the children of deportees admire their parents and want to hear their stories.[73] But 10 per cent of them have their suspicions and think that their fathers survived the camps because they collaborated with the enemy.[74] Identifying with parents who have been defeated leads to either low self-esteem or a desire for revenge. But not identifying with them leads to betrayal, shame and guilt. Children who have been wounded overcome the uneasiness they feel when they are told about their parents' ordeal by heightening their image of it. As they themselves did not experience the trauma and have no more than a few strange clues as to what happened, their pain or resistance has to do with the way it has been depicted. The parents suffered the blow, but the children have to deal with what they think of that blow.

Their respective pain simply cannot be handled in the same way. The parents suffered a real trauma, and defended themselves by mobilizing all the costly defences that could help lessen the pain. Their children, in contrast, are faced with a representation which, because it is stylized in the same way that a symbol or a working drawing is stylized, triggers much more intense emotions. They find it harder to defend themselves.

There are biological and psychological grounds for believing that, when the relatives of trauma victims share their emotions and feel their pain, they are often more damaged than the victims themselves.[75]

Their cortisol levels, the acorticoid receptors and the secretion of CRF (cortico-releasing factor) show that the children of parents who have been traumatized are chronically depressed. The anxiety-ridden environment in which they grow up constantly stimulates their emotions and eventually exhausts them. The fact that their brain receptors have become hypersensitive to any stimulation explains why these subjects experience banalities as a real form of aggression. Cortisol is the hormone that stimulates the adrenal cortex, and these children's cortisol levels are four times higher than those of the population at large.

The paradoxical thing about this impressive discovery is that a trauma victim is, in biological terms, better equipped to handle stress, in the same way that a trained athlete is better equipped to face up to a physical challenge. Emotional adaptation to a trauma is not a transient defence mechanism; it is an acquired biological reaction, 'the indelible imprint of a traumatic event'.[76] After an assault, the metamorphosis is biological. The victim has now acquired a way of experiencing the world and responding to it. Because he was wounded as a child, he has learned how to react. But because an imprint or trace has been implanted in his memory, he has also become hypersensitive to certain kinds of events. If something similar occurs forty years later, the superman might collapse when faced with a very minor ordeal that reminds him of the major assault.

For their part, the trauma victim's children are attached to a vulnerable champion who infects the people who love him with an emotional fever. They

experience a stress that has no face, a shapeless aggression on the part of this attachment figure. They feel
exhausted and are always anxious without knowing why.
They are constantly on the alert, but they do not know
for what. They do not know what to defend themselves
against, because they are under the impression that they
themselves are the source of the problem, and not those
they love. Suffering can only be transmitted between
people who are attached to one another and who are
able to empathize. A child who pays no attention to
what his mother is passing on will be better able to
protect himself than a child who is too attached and
who perceives the slightest emotional fluctuations.

Several thousand sets of identical twins fought in
Vietnam. Their biological, behavioural and emotional
closeness gave them an emotional style that could be
very quickly transmitted from one twin to the other.
'We understand each other perfectly,' they said. The
result of their great empathy was that, when one twin
was harmed emotionally, the twin who did not experience the traumatic event suffered to a much greater
extent. Similarly, the children of Holocaust survivors
are three times more likely to suffer from post-traumatic
stress disorder than their parents.[77]

It is not difficult to explain the psychic transmission
of organic disorders. Traumatized parents adapt to
their wounds by using defence mechanisms that are
costly but effective: splitting of the personality, denial

of memory, daydreaming as a form of compensation, activism and altruism are the classic examples. These defences organize a relational style based upon anger, anxious love, insane but necessary dreams or altruistic struggles, and their children become caught up in them. But the children cannot understand the anger, silences, desperate love and permanent mental fatigue of the parents they live with day by day. The problem has been passed on to them, but they have no perception of what is causing it. Whilst the wounded parents had to face up to reality, their children have to fight a ghost. 'The transmission is not based upon a content, but primarily on the act of transmitting.'[78] We do not have to speak in order to disturb those who love us. The trace of the traumatic event that lives on inside the psyche, inside a sort of ominous crypt, affects the behaviour and emotions of the wounded soul. In many cases, the deep part of the brain that controls emotions and memories is atrophied.[79] And that in turn affects those close to the sufferer.

Sharing our misfortunes means asking our families to fight our battles for us

A child who grows up in an emotional context like this inevitably becomes imprinted with the disturbed gestures that have escaped from his parents' secret history. He integrates them into his psyche and even his biology, and cannot really defend himself against them because he cannot identify his aggressor. He has only a few mysterious clues, and they are disguised by those he loves most.

Given that a secret is making both the wounded soul and those around him anxious, it seems only logical to conclude that revealing the secret is enough to make everything better. But the world has no common sense, and what looks reasonable to one person looks stupid to another. When the speaker tells the story of his sufferings, he is much more disturbed by the reaction of the person he is confiding in than by the evocation of his own wounds. When an adolescent who had survived the camps in Cambodia described the incredible horrors he had endured, he saw the look of disgust on his friend's face as he was saying 'I admire you for having survived all that.'

Sharing our misfortunes means changing those who are close to us. 'We are even unsure whether we have the right to talk about the events of our own lives.'[80] What right do we have to ruin our friends' dinner parties? What right do we have to talk about our sorrows to the people who want to make us happy? What makes me a spokesperson for the torments suffered by the disappeared? Not to mention the fact that, when I reveal how unhappy I am, there is a danger that I will become a prisoner of the very image

I have always fought. By revealing my secret, I force the people who love me to fight my battles for me. 'My mother was so ashamed of herself that I no longer even knew why I was ashamed of myself. We were never like other people. We had to be better,' explained a young woman who was active in a prisoners' welfare association. Guess why.

We forget that secrecy has a defensive function. When a victim reveals her secret she lays herself bare and exposes herself to the gaze of other people, who are sometimes eager to know more but who may also laugh at her. Once she lowers her guard, her story belongs to other people. We have confided in people who will laugh at us. We are no longer in control. What are we to do with our pain in a society that wants to use it, relativize it, laugh at it or make a drama of it? Whilst all we have to do to protect ourselves is keep the secret, revealing it is all it takes to make us vulnerable. That is why the ego has to spend thirty or even fifty years building up its strength before we can even put it into words.[81]

'Even': that is the problem. Because no society is capable of just listening. Secrecy is a necessity in a civilization that values individuality. But in a culture in which there is no such thing as an individual, there is no call for secrecy, as Orwell might have put it. All human groups where the individual is no more than a 'sub-self' detest secrecy.

Confessional cultures have no qualms about inflicting torture in the name of morality. One of the first best-sellers was the *Malleus maleficarum*, a volume which codified the torture techniques recommended by the Inquisition to extract confessions in order to ensure that everyone shared the same belief and that all 'sub-selves' were part of the same narrative. Ideological dictatorships have used various methods in an attempt to carry out the same project. Some insisted that everyone's papers were in order and made them declare their origins to ensure that the race was pure.[82] Others used sleep deprivation to ensure that the confessions they extracted were complete and that the social narrative was not disturbed by other ways of thinking. The purpose of these tortures was no secret: every individual had to be reduced to the role of a 'sub-self' to ensure that the group functioned as efficiently as possible and worshipped its leader, or the great 'super-self'.

Extorting confessions becomes a way of raping souls. The victims who were hurt by their assailants are tortured again by the social representatives who force them to become normal once again.

Abused children try to protect their mothers. 'I walked into a door' and 'I fell down the stairs' are the usual lies which, by saving their mothers' honour, allow them to feel a little less ashamed. Once the child has disclosed the aggression, all she can do is mourn her mother's love: 'That's it. I've disclosed how she used to torture me. She will never forgive me. By making the fact that she tortured me public knowledge, I've exposed myself to shame: I am the girl with a terrifying mother. No one will ever look at me the way they used to.' Once their ordeals have been exposed by compassionate souls, the children often feel more alone than ever and are extremely vulnerable because they have given in to the people who asked them to open the forbidden crypt. The social workers can go home once their job is done, but the children are left alone, naked and defenceless. They have lost all hope of ever establishing some bond, because, even in the depths of their emotional despair, there were still a few moments of happiness, – what David Bisson calls 'slices of paradise' – in the hell created by their mothers: 'I remember a parenthesis . . . I went out with my mother one day . . . We walked all day . . . I made her laugh. And she really did laugh.'[83] We need these islands of happiness in order to keep our hopes alive. And when confession simply means identifying the aggressor by exposing him or her to the public greed of right-thinking people, it destroys any hope of rehabilitation. If the victim is not to feel weakened by her confession she must have some external social support. She must also have internal psychological support. Before she can find that support, she must be able to feel strong.

Confession modifies our sense of self by changing the image we project into the minds of others. When a criminal feels guilty, confessing his crimes brings him relief, expiation makes him feel normal; but when a child discloses that he has been hurt by the people who should have protected him, he destroys other people's image of the ones he wanted to love. The child then becomes the aggressor ... and like the aggressor he is ashamed of. Even whilst they are being beaten and humiliated, many abused children despise their mothers not because they are hurting them but because they have no self-control. But when they disclose the abuse to right-thinking adults, who either react with horror or relish their tales of abuse, they are not only ashamed of having a mother who is not like other mothers, but also feel guilty because they have become aggressors in their turn and are just like the aggressors they despise. The confession becomes a sin, and the child punishes herself because she has had her mother punished.

It is not unusual for a child to want to rescue her aggressor or to want to preserve his image. So she lies in order to create a socially acceptable image in the minds of others. She invents an ideal father or a perfect mother, and dissociates him or her from the reality she is suffering in secret. 'It was a neighbour who pushed me down the stairs,' said one terribly damaged little girl. 'My parents forgot to leave me a key,' said the little boy whose parents had gone on holiday and deliberately locked him out so that he would not make a mess in the house. The lie protects the child because it offers other people an idealized picture of his parents, and because that allows him to go on thinking that he is, like all children, normal and has parents who are normal. 'So I am not the child of a monster.' The lie that preserves the image of the parents actually helps to protect the child's self-image.

The effect of revealing the secret depends upon who is listening, and upon how they feel about being a confidant

We have to be strong to allow ourselves to make a confession that destabilizes those around us. During the early years of her marriage, the father of Madame B's husband was her lover. She never spoke about this, but locking away the secret had a very serious effect on her relations with her family, who criticized her for her sullenness and inexplicable rages. Tortured by a past that haunted her, she eventually confessed to her husband, who killed himself.

Madame M was an incest victim for years until she found a job abroad in order to get away from her father. Having put some distance between them, she finally summoned up the courage to talk to an acquaintance, who immediately offered to help her. She was therefore very proud of 'having sent my father to prison', but her victory cost her dear. 'When I revealed my secret, I lost all my friends. You wash your dirty linen in private. I washed mine in public. My family has never forgiven me. I've been on my own ever since. My relations with them were never the same again.'

Carine wrote a book in order to exorcize her sexual relationship with her father. And then she married a nice young man and had a child by him. Her book was such a success that people sometimes stopped her in the street to ask her in front of her little girl, who was quite old enough to understand what was being said, 'And what about this child? Is she your father's?' 'The book is suffocating me. Now that I've revealed my secret, people keep stopping me from not thinking about what happened.'

Madame C barricaded herself in to escape from her father. 'I used to tell my lovers about it. They couldn't handle it. Now, I lie. I've met a man who also has a secret. It does me good to think that he suffered, just like me.' A secret that is shared becomes more bearable when the other person knows how to listen and knows not to give it away. Madame C liked being able to share her pain with her new lover. It allowed her to feel that she was his equal. She did not know his secret, but she no longer feels ashamed now that she is with him because his history also contains a painful mystery.

When Monsieur P told a colleague about how his mother used to make advances towards him, he saw the mocking glint in his colleague's eye. He immediately began to hate the man in whom he had just confided. 'I needed to say it. But as soon as I saw his expression change, I realized that he was laughing at my shame, and I hated him. I now feel uncomfortable when anyone who knows looks at me. I feel even more ashamed than ever.'

Talking about our pain is not enough to settle all our scores with the past. The reactions of the person to whom the secret is disclosed has an influence on the psyche of the one who is revealing it. That is why disclosing a secret can both bring relief and be a form of torture. It is not unusual for a victim to talk about the horrors of his or her tragedy for the first time on television. Paradoxically, this public act is far from being indecent; it is an intimate act. 'When I tried to talk to my grandmother about it, she shut me up. My neighbours told me I was lying, that my father was a good man. On television, at least I can be sure I'm talking to people who can understand me.' Because she wants intimacy, she talks to an audience of eight million.

In order to understand this dilemma, a population of wounded souls who had revealed their tragedies was compared with an identical population that had kept quiet about them. The answer was clearly that there was

no difference between them.[84] The fact that the populations were identical certainly does not mean, however,
that keeping quiet about their secrets or revealing them
did not affect the individuals concerned. Some felt better
and some felt worse, which indicates that, whilst the
proportional figures did not change, all the individuals
who made up the populations did. That is what the
figures tell us. And when a secret is involved, what they
tell us is even less clear. But the findings of the study
lead the authors to conclude that 'Children who do not
disclose, or who do not disclose immediately, present
fewer symptoms than those who do.'[85] The 'not immediately' is important because it testifies to the need to
take into account when the disclosure is made, when the
wounded soul felt strong enough to talk about it, and
whether or not the historical context gave the listener
enough hindsight to listen to him or her. A victim who
feels an inner compulsion to bear witness usually remains
silent when her social group shuts her up. How can
anyone talk to their own daughter? How can anyone
talk to her about how he suffered during the war when,
forty years later, she admits, 'I didn't want to know. I
was afraid of commemorating the nightmare.'[86] Given
that we know that this mental damage is contagious, we
cannot criticize the victims' children for trying to defend
themselves. But when emotional closeness brings down
the barriers, even more damage is done.

Martine was six when her father came back from

the camps. She was truly frightened as she listened to her father, who was all skin and bones, telling his terrifying stories: 'He told us those stories on purpose, just to hurt us. I held that against him. So I didn't listen.'

When Pierrot joined the resistance at the age of sixteen, he was the only living survivor of his family. The rest were all dead. After the war he continued to be politically active and regularly invited old resisters aged between thirteen and thirty home. Their children played together, and wallowed in their stories of death, torture, lynchings and denunciations. Thirty years later, almost all those children were suffering from post-traumatic stress disorder. They were fascinated by death, conspiracies and injustice, and their nights were tormented by constant anxieties. They had difficulty in identifying the source of their problems because they loved their parents and had been affected by the same violence. But they and their parents did not experience that violence in the same way: Pierrot and his friends were evoking tragedies that had, with hindsight, become victories, whereas their children experienced only the horror.

During the war Agnès was happy with her mother and her two little sisters. But when her father, who had been deported for political reasons, came home, he never stopped talking about the heaps of corpses, about the fluid that oozed from them, and about the friends who died during the morning roll call. For more than thirty years Agnès trembled with fear when anything new happened. Every night she looked under her bed for the pile of corpses. She thought she could smell them in her bedroom and expected her family to die.

All these fathers had suffered during the war, but they had held their own. They survived. Once peace was restored, they fought the temptation to deny their past and to use splitting mechanisms by telling graphic stories about the ordeals they had been forced to endure. But their children kept asking themselves why they found life in a world that was at peace so difficult, when their fathers had triumphed over so many horrors. The fathers' careless talk of victories had imbued their children's minds with a feeling of low self-esteem.

We cannot say everything. Only psychotics and perverts say whatever comes into their heads, and that is because they are indifferent to the effect their words will have on the mental worlds of other people. How can anyone say to their daughter, as Madame F did, 'It was the other one who died. Your sister. I'd rather it had been you'? How can we understand the desire to decorate the house of the woman who abused us in order to win her over and 'prove to her that she was wrong not to love me'? How can we understand the astonishing sentence 'I hate him so much that I would give anything to make him love me'?[87]

If we are not to become strangers to ourselves, those around us must allow our ego to do some body-building

I speak so as to cease being a stranger to myself, but when I do so, I change other people's mental image of me, and I do not know what they are going to do with that image. I express myself so as to imprint myself on other people. But telling myself the story of my sufferings night after night in my own words has no effect on public representations. It is only when I confide in someone that I appear before the court of other people. When I confide my secret, I hope that the shared intimacy will change other people's world of representations and their image of me. They do not have to answer me in words. They can remain silent, but the way they remain silent must mean, 'I accept you and your secret. And that will bind us together from now on.'

Speaking to large numbers of people, in contrast, and divulging one's secrets to them is not a way of sharing them. It is a way of exposing oneself, in the way that we expose ourselves to blows, or in the sense of giving an exposé. Divulging one's secret in public means choosing one's clan, assuming we have one. When we open up to ourselves, we are at our most vulnerable. Sharing a secret is an intimate act that creates a bond: a secret that is made public represents a social commitment.

There is no shortage of social disasters to confirm this thesis. We simply have to look at them fairly carefully.[88] In 1947 a population of 412 Russian Jews who had been shattered by the war split into two groups of immigrants. The incidence of depression and anxiety disorders in the group that settled in Israel, where their stories were accepted – and I do mean 'accepted' in the narrowest of senses, and without any emphasis on commiseration – was low. The rest of the population, who had suffered the same history, settled in the United States, where, like all the immigrants of the day, they were left to their own devices. Little was said to them, and they had few friends and received little help. The incidence of depression was much higher in this group.[89] When we try to identify the category with the highest incidence of depression, we find that it comprises the elderly, widows and divorcees, in other words people who are on their own and who are not part of a speech network. Confiding in someone, in the banal sense of the term, has an astonishing power to protect, provided that the subject who confides the secret feels that he or she is speaking in confidence. And that implies that family and friends, and especially the society in which they live, must provide a sympathetic environment.[90] The incidence of depression among women who had the support of husbands, families and friends was ten times lower than among women who were on their own and who had experienced the same violence in Russia.

The powerful tranquillizing effect of speech depends largely upon the empathy of the listener. Because of his emotional attitude and the social representation he embodies, he makes it possible for the wounded soul to express himself. Chemical tranquillizers certainly provide relief, but they act less rapidly than the effect of speech. What is more, this chemically induced relief lasts for only a few hours, but once we have confided our secret and tried to understand our suffering, we are no longer the same. We have undergone a metamorphosis.

When the wounded soul once more becomes coherent and whole because he feels that he has been accepted, along with this past, those around him also experience an astonishing feeling of relief. When the crypt has been opened, the ghosts go back to where they came from. The incidence of psychological disorders in one population of 2,000 high-school students in Jerusalem whose parents were deported was no higher than in the overall population.[91] The same is not true of a similar population of children in Paris.[92] Almost all their wounded parents, who had been reduced to silence by a culture that could not understand their tragedy, passed on their anxiogenic secrets. And almost all the wounded parents who were forced to talk about it by a culture that exploited their sufferings passed on their traumatic anxiety.

When the Russian war veterans, most of whom were aged between thirty and forty, came back from Afghanistan, their society silenced them with great cruelty. They had left home as young men to fight in a meaningless war, and they came home mutilated, amputated, traumatized. They were forced to remain silent. They were given no invalidity pensions, no free health care, and no awards for courage, and no attempt was made to resocialize them. Like the young Americans who came back from Vietnam and who wanted to bear witness, they were silenced by the population and by doctors who accused them of lying or simulating.[93]

The social fraud that sends young men off to be killed and to suffer so much and then abandons them and silences them to stop them embarrassing those who stayed at home is strongly reminiscent of the story of the forgotten men who served in the French 'policing operation' in Algeria. No one talked about a war and no one opened health centres for them. No one helped them, and they were even accused of having gone on holiday to defend the settlers. It is not just that they were on their own. What made their suffering, and that of their families, even worse is that, as is usual in such cases, negationists ridiculed their suffering.

We are treating the wrong patient: if we want the wounded to feel less pain, we must treat not them but our culture

All these accounts lead me to suggest that, if the wounded are to stop suffering, if the amputees are to walk again and if those around them are to stop feeling an anxiety that comes from beyond, we have to bring about a cultural shift.

Creativity is a defensive reaction that encourages the victims of aggression to bounce back. It is a fine tool, and it encourages them to become part of a cultural adventure. If they remain silent, we find them strange and say that they are 'deceitful', but when they do speak, some kind souls allude to the commercialization of their sufferings. Torn between the internal constraints that force them to speak and the external force that obliges them to keep quiet, damaged souls often discover that creativity is their best means of expression.

I am not attempting to explain away the creative genius, but we can demonstrate 'what motive forces aroused it and what material was offered ... by destiny'.[94] It is easy to see creativity as a heaven-sent gift, as an almost divine act or as some kind of super-natural 'psyche-plus', and to say that creative people are almost superhuman. But on the contrary, it is loss, absence and mourning that force the wounded to fill the void with representations to avoid feeling anxious about death and nothingness, zero and infinity. It is in the vertiginous void created by loss that symbols create the representations that can replace the lost object. Stylized images and words fill the void created by loss. Bringing the dead back to life and helping the wounded to enjoy life once more 'are present at the cradle of human culture', as André Haynal puts it.[95]

The image was born of the struggle against the despair caused by the ultimate loss: death. That is why the earliest forms of civilized art were on tombs, and why paintings later depicted entombments and resurrections. Images allow us to bring back to life the dead person whose image is still alive deep inside us. That is why, when he attended his wife's funeral, Prince Rainier of Monaco could not take his eyes off the photograph of the woman whose body lay in the coffin beside him. By staring intently at the dead woman's face, he could transform the despair he felt at losing her into the painful pleasure of making her live a little longer.

It is our fear of the dark that encourages us to light up unknown worlds. It was our fear that our mother would leave us that led us to pretend our teddy bears could talk when we were little, just as it is our fear that we will be hurt again that encourages us to make the effort to ensure that we are not. The suffering caused by absence and the pain of loss forces us to use symbols. Art can bring the dead back to life, just as philosophy can bandage wounds. It is remarkable how many creative people were orphaned or separated from their parents as children.[96] Balzac, Gérard de Nerval, Victor Hugo, Baudelaire, Alexandre Dumas, Stendhal and more than half the great writers of the nineteenth century confirm this theory. The act of creation closes a gap, heals wounds and allows us to become ourselves once more, to become our complete selves. Mourning and creativity are closely linked because anyone who has lost something or someone is forced to create an image of the thing or person he can no longer see. Creativity is not a cerebral or molecular aptitude, as it is completely bound up with the life history of the wounded artist, who must, if he is to save his own life, restore the lost object and 'be reconciled with death'.[97]

Perhaps that is why a wound that makes us grit our teeth becomes a form of theatre as soon as we can put it into words. Putting our sufferings into words almost always respects the rules of the well-made play:[98]

- The author states his narrative identity: 'I am the Count of Monte Cristo. I am the man who was wrongly imprisoned.'
- Action: 'I was in the Château d'If, a prison surrounded by the sea, when, suddenly . . .'

- Goal: 'I want to avenge myself, twenty years later.'
- Scene: 'Come in, come in and you will see what I did to take my revenge on the upwardly mobile bourgeoisie of the nineteenth century.'
- Instrument: 'My social success will be my way of punishing them.'

All these ingredients are there in the real world and they make it possible to stage a play about how the hero emerged triumphant from his ordeal. The theme of the play or novel is, in fact, supplied by the disaster itself. As Sartre remarks of Genet, genius is not a gift but the way out we find in desperate cases. The play or novel retraces in detail the story of a liberation.[99]

Nothing has changed. This is a basic defence mechanism that has been used ever since human beings began to think about death and to use works of art to resist it. 'Some people still ask whether poetry can exist after Auschwitz ... In the face of those claiming it cannot be done, survivors blessed with literary ability feel compelled to record their stories ... they have to bear witness for the other, in order to save them from their anonymous fate ... the urgency they feel to give the dead a narrative voice recreates poetry ... without art, that is, without poetry, the possibility of understanding what went on in Auschwitz or Kolyma would be closed to us for ever.'[100] Any struggle against death

– in other words, any consciousness of being alive – forces us to write poetry. To cite Solzhenitsyn, 'Art . . . recreates – lifelike – the experience of other men, so that we can assimilate it as our own.'[101]

Jean-Paul Sartre, Alain Finkielkraut and Aleksandr Solzhenitsyn are all agreed that wounded souls have the right to speak. But a purely clinical case history or a crude description is not enough to heal the wounds and to bring the dead back to life.

The name of the character who tried the experiment was called Punchinello. Before this joker was born in Naples in 1649, everyone could see that his mother's belly was swelling. She was the only one who could not see what was really going on. The neighbours swore she had a bun in the oven [*un polichinelle dans le tiroir*]. Mother Punchinello gave her baby up as soon as he was born, and he suffered depression as a very young boy. His growth was stunted and he failed to put on weight. He also developed kyphoscoliosis, or a pronounced curvature of the spine. Because he had never known a mother's love, the boy was convinced that no woman would ever love him. And so, in order to prove himself wrong, whenever he saw a woman, he dressed up in a grotesque costume and danced in front of her as he played his mandolin, explains Michel Soulé.[102] Being entirely unconcerned about the effect his words might have on others, Punchinello said the first thing that came into his head. In his view, all truths should come out. He was beaten so many times because of what he revealed that he resolved to keep quiet but, because he could not keep a secret, he also let slip some clue that revealed the mystery. Eventually, everyone was talking about the secret. [*Le secret de Polichinelle* is the French equivalent of 'an open secret.' DM]

Much the same thing happens today: as soon as a victim is forced to reveal her secret, it becomes even more oppressive. For those around her, she becomes 'the woman who was raped'; the rape 'explains' her whole personality and even her history: 'Once I admitted that I was an incest victim, I became "the woman who was the incest victim". And I've been stuck with that reputation ever since; it's much worse than when I kept it secret,' I was told by a young woman who had become the victim of her revelation's literary success.

So how can we filter our emotions so as to satisfy so many contradictory needs? As Jewish writer, activist and Holocaust survivor Elie Wiesel puts it, 'I have been forbidden to remain silent, it is impossible for me to speak.'[103] If I remain silent, my secret splits me and amputates part of me, just as it does emotional damage to the people who love me. But when I talk about it openly, describe what happened to me and the way I felt, I am stigmatized by other people's stories. I am alienated by their gaze and become more

vulnerable than ever. And so, in order to avoid 'the
scandal of their silence . . . I write: I write because we
lived together, because I was one amongst them, a
shadow amongst their shadows, a body close to their
bodies. I write because they left in me their indelible
mark, whose trace is writing. Their memory is dead
in writing; writing is the memory of their death and
the assertion of my life,' writes Georges Perec, who
was both in pain and happy.[104]

*It is said that creativity is the daughter of
suffering; this does not mean that suffering
is the mother of creativity*

Why does this defence come so easily to the minds of
abused children? Young children draw, and older children write. The pen and pencil do more to defend us
than activism, vengeance, isolation or regression. Writing condenses a great number of defence mechanisms
– intellectualization, daydreaming, rationalization and
sublimation – into a single activity. It allows us to assert
ourselves and, at the same time, to identify ourselves,
to inscribe ourselves in a glorious lineage and, above
all, to be accepted for what we are, wounds and all.
Every writer is addressing an ideal reader.

Is creativity the daughter of suffering?[105] Do our
torments inspire works of art? They say that a young

man once asked André Gide, 'What should I do to become a writer?' 'Go and work in a factory,' replied the master. Happiness produces nothing but blank sheets of paper. But will surviving an ordeal really make a book, or even a chapter?

A group of women writers met to discuss this idea.[106] Fifty-nine women belonging to a writers' association were interviewed, and their answers were compared with those given by a second small group of women of the same age, with similar levels of education and from similar backgrounds but who were not writers. Personality profiles, an evaluation of the diagnostic criteria and information about their lifestyles were used to look at the possible comparisons. An analysis of the findings revealed that the incidence of mental disorders was twice as high in the writers' group. There were no psychotics in the little group; anyone who wants to write a book has to be able to plan ahead, accumulate notes and remain in control of reality. Fifty-six per cent of the group did, on the other hand, suffer from recurrent depression and various forms of anxiety (chronic or violent). There were many cases of eating disorders, such as anorexia and bulimia, and of drug and alcohol abuse.

An identical study of a group of male writers produced similar findings, but there was a higher incidence of alcoholism and mood swings. Most of the wounds that are inflicted on the psyche are inflicted by the family or social environment, and the researchers discovered a regular pattern when they looked at the subjects' backgrounds: many of the women writers had been sexually abused as girls. Most members of both groups had suffered some form of abuse. Many had loved mothers who were mentally ill. The fact that they had a score to settle or felt an inner compulsion to talk about their tragedies forced them to be creative and become prolific writers. This does not mean that the reverse is true: you do not have to have been abused to become a creator.

We do not really know what makes a child suffer. The fact that nothing bad happens in an overprotected environment creates a situation of emotional confinement that makes children vulnerable to anything new. An adult would not find such an environment traumatic, but it represents a real ordeal for a child. Proust and Freud both began to write after the deaths of their fathers because the disappearance of an overpowering image imprinted on them a sensation of loss that forced them to be creative. It is as though the sudden absence of a father took a weight off the shoulders of these children, who had everything they could wish for, and forced them to fill the void by creating other images, in the same way that the death of a loved one encourages us to invent rituals and build tombs. The pain of loss does much more than the pain inflicted by blows to make artists of us. Chateaubriand suffered because of his harsh education, but it was not the suffering that made him a creative writer; it was the melancholy it induced that made him so isolated. 'What is certain is that it was [this harsh education] that imprinted melancholy characteristics on my feelings. Those characteristics were born of my habitual suffering at an age when I was weak, had no foresight, and was happy,' he wrote. Talleyrand also remembered that 'I felt lonely and had no support ... it was my earliest thoughts ... that got me into the habit of thinking more deeply than I might have done if I had had only minor reasons to be happy.'[107]

Insane dreams can make up for a loss: dream or die

This explains why children who have an abandonment neurosis because they were separated from their mothers and placed in institutional care at a very early age desperately need to invent mother substitutes: 'I used to have a mum too' allows a child to tell itself, 'I am like other children.' And the common game of 'You look like my mum' likewise allows them to feel that they once had a mother. A child who does have parents will play 'mummy and daddy', but a little orphan has to imagine a stage production in which another adult looks 'like my mum'. In order to create a mother substitute, she writes a play in two acts. The first act allows her to feel safe within an internal world that is at peace, and the second allows her to get over the inevitable separation.[108] Reconstructing the maternal object cancels out the separation. The effect is immediate: creating an imaginary object calms the child down, and she very quickly learns to love it. These little creators often say, 'I love dreaming . . . I love writing . . . I love making up plays.' But whilst it does give them pleasure, this defence sets a relational trap for them because the child gives the other woman the power to be a mother, to take the place of her real mother. And in the real world, not all women want to be mothers, or at least not just mothers. Having invented a mother in her inner theatre, the child will now have to find another one when she is older. Imagining she has a mother allows her to bear the loss of her real mother, but as she grows up, the deprived girl will have to learn to establish a different relationship with one particular woman. As she has never learned how to love a real mother, she is always forced to create and to learn. She does so in her imaginary world before applying what she knows to the real world. Her psychological development is quite different from that of a normal girl.

Little Stanislas was four during the Second World War. One night, he went to bed in his lovely house. When the noise of the bombing woke him up, the

roof had fallen in and his family had disappeared. He
was quite astonished to find that he felt no pain. He
felt a little ashamed of still being alive and was disoriented by the silence that followed the racket and
by the immense feeling of emptiness that surrounded
him. It was not worth calling out, crying or even
looking around for someone. There was no one. For
a long time he lay on his back, staring into the void.
He lay like that for three years, not speaking but just
surviving. He was almost seven when the rebuilding
of Warsaw began. The builders had started by putting
up wooden stage sets to show people what they were
going to build. The sets awakened little Stanislas's
hopes. He thought to himself, 'It will be the same for
me.' And so he began to have incredible dreams.
'When I'm grown up, I will do this and that.' He began
to talk to himself and to recount his daydreams which,
like the painted stage sets of Warsaw, gave him hope.
He became incredibly euphoric. The real world that
had been shattered was of secondary importance now.
Stanislas was walking on air and smiled sweetly
because he was living inside the dreams he was always
inventing. When he was placed in a cold, desolate
institution that had taken in a thousand children, he
scarcely suffered at all. There were so few members
of staff to look after the children that not one adult
spoke to him for several years. The only way they
related to the children was by hitting them to make

them walk in line, barefoot in the snow, on their compulsory excursions. The meals they were given in the vast, noisy refectory were inadequate. All the children wanted to be 'table monitors' because the child who wiped the table with a damp rag at the end of each meal could grab an extra handful of crumbs and scraps of food. For Stanislas the leftovers were a real treat, a happy event, and something of a joke. At night the dormitory, with its 100 beds, was freezing. The only monitor, whose bed was separated from the children's dormitory by a sheet, established a reign of terror so as to get to sleep a little earlier. Stanislas really loved being alone in his icy bed because, as he drifted off to sleep, he knew he had a date with his dreams.

Almost all resilient children who are happy in a world that is cold, desolate and hungry survive thanks to the extraordinary power of daydreaming to make us feel warm. These moments of happiness, which are cut off from the real world, always involve images from the same type of scenario: the child is alone in a world of hostile adults, but has discovered a wonderful hiding place. It is part of an emotional paradise. Every night Stanislas wandered through a leafless forest of wicked trees. They tried to catch him and hurt him with their clawed branches. But the boy knew that there was an invisible door in a hollow tree. He went down a little tunnel and there, deep underground, far away from the world of men, wonderful animals were waiting for him, each more beautiful than the rest. And then the party began. There were frolicking deer, funny sleigh dogs and even aquariums that lit up the underground world with thousands of bright colours.

Twenty years later, little Serban discovered the same defence mechanism in his orphanage in Romania, while living in a sixty-bedded room where no one ever spoke. Some of his comrades rocked constantly and, every time they rocked, their beds moved a few millimetres forward. At night the women who had been sentenced to looking after the children as a punishment, began to shout because the beds had moved right across the big room. Serban refused to wash his backside because the faecal crust that had dried on him meant that he would not be raped. And yet he was always smiling because, in his inner world, he was living in a blue lagoon. He would set off in his canoe and head for a place that only he knew about. He dived and went through the two airlocks that stood between him and the water, and suddenly he was under a sort of glass canopy. It was warm and brightly coloured, and he was surrounded by strange but wonderful animals. And then the party began.

Freud thought that a happy man did not need to dream and that reality was enough to keep him satisfied. Sartre evokes the 'essential poverty' of the dream object, which is always on the point of vanishing.[109] But Bachelard, like little Stanislas and little Serban, took the view that 'the man of reverie bathes in the happiness of dreaming the world, bathes in the well-being of a happy world'.[110]

This is, of course, an escape from reality, but when the real world has gone mad, we have to protect ourselves from it. Only children who can dream can save themselves. The others, who have adapted to the real world and surrendered to a ravaged world, are inundated with pieces of information that are bleak, poor, immediate and, therefore, devoid of meaning. Despair is the appropriate response to a world like this. We cannot create poetry with indices and signals. We need symbols, images and stories if the representations we create are to warm us up by inducing a sense of beauty, and even happiness. Stanislas and Serban did more than learn to tolerate a desolate real world thanks to their dreams. They overinvested in a world of wonders. Their world was split into a real world where adaptation meant despondency, and an inner world that was warm, colourful and loving. That is why both boys went to sleep with a smile on their lips: they were going to meet their dreams in a dormitory that was full of nightmares.

All deprived children live in an environment that has been marked by loss, and in which vagueness is an invitation to be creative. 'That mindless mist where shadows whirl, how could I pierce it?' asks Raymond Queneau, whose words provide the epigraph to Perec's *W*. Children who survive in a mindless mist are forced to go in search of treasure; their only alternative is to succumb to despair. But those who have a clear parental reference have a star to guide them. At first they follow it, and then it becomes imprinted on them. But when they reach adolescence and want to become themselves, they have to rebel against it, which is, of course, another way of identifying with it. 'We become adults the day we do what we want to do, even if it makes our parents unhappy,' as Paul Watzlawick puts it.[111]

Deprived children whose origins lie in the shadows are forced to write a painful poetry, a poetry in which beauty rubs shoulders with ugliness and in which inner happiness coexists with unhappiness.

Having to blossom on a knife edge is not necessarily a disadvantage, as too much light can dazzle us and because children who have exceptional parents and an imposing lineage are alienated by a forced identification that leaves no room for the imagination. 'In our family, we have been shopkeepers from one generation to the next.' A message like that helps children to develop, but then imprisons them because its structure forces them to keep going in the same direction.

Those who have been wounded by life are forced to discover 'places where they can cheat',[112] or an island that exists in an inner world. The island is warm, even though it does not speak any language that would allow it to communicate with the outside world. It is there that they learn how to compromise and to speak despite everything. 'I write because [my parents] left in me their indelible mark, whose trace is writing.'[113] For those who have experienced a desolate childhood, writing is a way of giving shape to words that cannot be spoken and of leaving a material trace on the outside world: 'Silence, sudden icy silence. There could be no survivor ... Whatever may happen now, I was the sole depository, the only vestige of that world. That, more than any other consideration, was what made me decide to write ... Writing is the memory of their death and the assertion of my life.'[114]

IV

Conclusion

Resilience means more than the ability to resist. It also means learning how to live. Unfortunately, there is a high price to be paid. 'One does not become normal with impunity,' said Cioran,[1] who knew a lot about how difficult it is to live. Before the disaster occurs, we believe that life – and happiness – is something that is owed to us. And so, when we do not achieve ecstasy, we get angry. The fact of having suffered as a result of some extreme situation, of having come close to death and having killed death triggers a strange feeling of relief in the soul of the wounded child: 'Since then, I have come to see life as something extra, as a joke that invites me to make the most of every moment and to savour my happiness.' When we have survived the ordeal, life tastes different, '[B]ecause it is a process that destroys life, any extreme situation contains, paradoxically, a potential for life . . . an invisible spring allows us to bounce back from the ordeal by turning the obstacle into a trampoline, fragility into wealth, weakness into strength, and impossibilities into a set of possibilities.'[2]

All disasters result in a metamorphosis. Those whose souls have been badly wounded or who have been mutilated by emotional deprivation, the children who have been battered and the adults who have been

flayed alive are living proof of the subjective emergence of a new philosophy of life. Because they are
under an obligation to understand and to ask 'Why?',
they learn and become better at analysing their aggressors. And the very fact of saying to themselves, 'And
what am I going to do with my wound now?' encourages them to discover the healthy part of themselves
and to go in search of whatever help they can find.

That is how resilience is knitted. Resilience is not
just something we find inside ourselves or in our environment. It is something we find midway between the
two, because our individual development is always
linked to our social development.

Coining neologisms is not a pointless exercise: it is a
way of fighting words that have become worn out and
theories that have seized up. Novel concepts oblige us
to refine our old concepts: because we can use the metaphor of knitting to describe resilience, we can do away
with the notion of individual strengths and weaknesses.
Resilience has nothing to do with vulnerability or invulnerability, and is quite different from the psychoanalytic
mechanism of resistance, which denies us access to the
unconscious, but it may have something in common with
the notion that the ego's defences have to be supported
by something. Psychoanalytic theory has elaborated the
notions of denial, splitting, human activism and many
other defence mechanisms, but the notion of resilience
places the emphasis on the ego's ability to adapt and

evolve. We can be resilient in one situation but not in another. We can be wounded one moment and victorious the next.

The ego uses its defence mechanisms to try to preserve its integrity by exploiting its intellectual and emotional resources, but there is always a physical dimension to them. Sigmund Freud and Anna Freud have shown us how the ego controls the drives and the way they represent our recollections and fantasies. Internal excitement gives the ego a form that we can tolerate. The work of the drives is therefore unconscious, and the conscious ego gives our emotions a verbal form by rationalizing them.

According to resilience theory, the damage is done by external rather than internal factors, but the ego that experiences it must still be in control of the emotional upheaval it causes. When the organism suffers emotional damage as a result of social violence or the mental violence inflicted by other people, stress is part of the shock. The stress is usually chronic, and its insidious effect damages both the organism and the psyche, which do not understand what is happening.

In all these cases, the feeling of selfhood, which is shaped by the gaze of others, can be reshaped and reworked by representations, actions, commitments and narratives. The concept of resilience, which has nothing to do with invulnerability, is one of the family of 'defence mechanisms'. It is, however, more conscious and more malleable than the other defences. It can therefore be controlled and can bring us happiness.

Not being made of steel and not being superhuman, resilient individuals cannot avoid this oxymoron. The pearl inside the oyster might be the emblem of resilience. When a grain of sand gets into an oyster and is so irritating that, in order to defend itself, the oyster has to secrete a nacreous substance, the defensive reaction produces a material that is hard, shiny and precious.

Anthony Bloom's notion of the 'damaged icon' illustrates how the souls of these individuals are made more beautiful by the wounds inflicted by time.[3] What remains is beautiful, and its beauty may even have been enhanced, despite the splinters of wood, the fading of the colours and the rotten knots.

Clinical research is often undertaken outside the laboratory or the consulting room. Which does not mean that one domain is better than the other. It was not until after the French Revolution that anyone thought of integrating medicine and surgery. As long as the verbal arrogance of doctors allowed them to despise the unskilled barber-surgeons, medicine remained verbose and surgery remained stereotypical. It was the coming together of the two that permitted the rise of medical semiology. The science of signs went on developing until the scientists and engineers took over. We can now do amazing things.

The purpose of this book was simply to say that

there is such a thing as resilience. Resilience has a form, and there is a price to be paid. All the researchers and practitioners who developed the concept are now looking at how resilience itself develops. Current research suggests that genetics may have a contribution to make. But early interactions will make their presence felt much later, when family and social institutions are doing most of the talking.

The knowledge we have acquired in the field and in the laboratory will be of use to us in our day-to-day lives because we are all resilient and because none of us has the good fortune to avoid pain completely.

I could, finally, have written this book with just three words: 'Bouncing back' and 'knitting'. 'Bouncing back' is a good description of resilience, whilst 'knitting' explains how we survive, just as the notion of a damaged icon describes the inner world of these wounded winners.

And so, we change the way we look at our sufferings and go in search of wonders despite the pain.

Acknowledgements

The concept of resilience is currently having a major impact on the British and American literature on the developmental sciences.

The concept was developed by psychiatrists and psychologists such as Michael Rutter in London and E. E. Werner, N. Garmery and G. E. Vaillant in the United States.

Their work is supported by the experimental observations of ethologists and the theories of evolutionary psychology and adaptation developed by John Bowlby, René Spitz, L. Soufre, J. Suomi, Mary Ainsworth and E. Tronick.

A. S. Masten was one of the first to establish the link between resilience and humour, whilst E. Grotberg reintroduced optimism into psychology.

Psychoanalysts paved the way: M. Mahler, Anna Freud and L. Shengold outlined a developmental approach to psychopathology by studying development mentors rather than symptoms. This approach was validated in the field of child psychiatry by clinicians such as E. J. Anthony and C. Chiland.

B. Inhelder has applied Piaget's theories to atypical development, as have cognitive psychologists, clinical psychologists, psychiatrists, neurologists and paediatricians such as D. Fostadter, B. Kapla, C. Izard, D. Cicceti, J. Kaga, J. Bruner, J. Rolf, S. Weintraub and A. Sameroff.

In Québec, the concept has been extended thanks to M. Lemay and M. Toussigant.

In England, P. Fonagy is currently working on resilience in young infants. Similar work is being done in France by A. Guedeny of the World Association of Infant Mental Health under the leadership of S. Lebovici and B. Wolse.

In the Netherlands, the Fondation Van Leer was one of the first institutions to support specialist field work on the resilience of young children in Africa and Latin America.

A. Haynal in Switzerland, F. Lösel in Germany and C. Badoura in Lebanon are working on the resilience of older children.

In Switzerland, S. Vanistendael and the BICE (Bureau International Catholique de l'Enfance) developed the concept of resilience by taking their inspiration from scientists and practitioners in various countries.

In Geneva. M. McCallin has brought together clinicians from the battlefields of the many continents where children are paying the price for the absurd crimes committed by adults.

Many practitioners are applying the concept of resilience in Latin America. They include M. A. Kotliarenco and S. Romero (Chile), N. S. Suarez Ojeda (Argentina), S. Panez (Peru) and C. Montevicente (Brazil).

In France, researchers and clinicians such as M. Manciaux, S. Tomkeiwicz, M. Duyne, N. Outre du Pasquier, A. Dumaret and the present author are working along similar lines.

The practitioners and field workers receive support from the following international organizations: Enfants Réfugiés du Monde and M. R. Moro, Ligue Roumaine de Santé Mentale and A. Pidolle, Médecins du Monde and Médicins Sans Frontières.

Many international institutions have become involved in this research in the course of their usual activities: UNICEF (Comité Français pour le Fonds des Nations Unies pour l'Enfance), Fondation pour l'Enfance, Enfance Majuscule and Ligue Française pour la Santé Mentale are financing concrete research projects and organizing seminars to make the concept of resilience more usable.

Several American journals have devoted special issues to resilience, including the *American Journal of Psychiatry*, the *Journal of Consulting and Clinical Psychology* and the *Journal of the American Academy of Child and*

Adolescent Psychiatry. One new journal is devoted exclusively to resilience: *Development and Psychopathology.*

It has, unfortunately, been impossible to cite all the authors, articles and books that currently deal with this problem. That is a pity, but it is also a clear indication of the importance of the concept of resilience. This developmental approach makes it possible to integrate different disciplines such as the neurosciences, psychology, genetics and behavioural studies by emphasizing the psychoanalytic, Piagetian and psycho-sociological approaches.

This inclusive approach allows us to avoid dualism, which is incompatible with a holistic approach to the clinical study of human beings. It also introduces a note of hope into the psychological sciences.

Notes

I Introduction: Resilience as a natural process

1 A. Ferran, Introduction to Charles Baudelaire, *Petits poèmes en prose*, Paris: Hachette, 1951.

2 Catherine Enjolet, *En Danger de silence*, Paris: Robert Laffont, 1999, p. 9.

3 S. Vanistendael, *Clés pour devenir: la résilience* (conference 'Les Vendredis de Châteauvallon', Nov. 1998), Les Cahiers du BICE, Geneva: Bureau International Catholique de l'Enfance, 1996, p. 9.

4 H. Malot, *Sans Famille*, Paris: Hachette, 1933.

5 Charles Dickens, Preface to *Oliver Twist*, London: Everyman, 1960, pp. xix, xxi.

6 H. Juin, Preface to L. Tolstöi, *Jeunesse, suivie de souvenirs*, Paris: Livre de Poche, 1971, p. 13.

7 Rudyard Kipling, 'If', in *A Choice of Kipling's Verse*, ed. T. S. Eliot, London: Faber & Faber, 1962, p. 274.

8 Jules Renard, *Carrots*, trans. G. W. Stonier, London: Grey Walls Press, 1946.

9 Hervé Bazin, *Grasping the Viper*, trans. W. J. Strachan, London: Secker & Warburg, 1950.

10 Jean-Luc Lahaye, *Cent familles*, Paris: Editions Carrère, 1985. Lahaye was born in Paris, but his precise date of birth is uncertain. In 1986, he founded the charity Cent Familles, which runs safe houses for children whose parents cannot look after them. [DM]

11 Dominique Lapierre, *The City of Joy*, trans. Kathryn Spink, Garden City, NY: Doubleday, 1985.

12 B. Rapp, personal communication about 'kids in Bogotá', 1998.

13 Anna Freud and Dorothy Burlingham, *Infants without Families: The Case for and against Residential Nurseries*, London: George Allen & Unwin, 1944; Anna Freud, *Normality and Pathology in Childhood*, London: Hogarth Press/Institute of Psychoanalysis, 1966.

14 Françoise Dolto, *La Difficulté de vivre*, Paris: Carrère, 1987.

15 M. Rutter, 'Psychosocial Resilience and Protective Mechanisms', in Jon Rolf and Ann Master, eds., *Risk and Protective Factors in the Development of Psychopathology*, New York: Cambridge University Press, 1990.

16 S. Ionescu, M.-M. Jacquet and C. Lhote, *Les Mécanismes de défense: théorie et clinique*, Paris: Nathan Université, 1997.

17 François Billetdoux, cited in G. Roux and M. Laharie, *L'Humour, histoire, culture et psychologie*, Pau: Société Internationale de Psychologie de l'Expression et de l'Art-Thérapie, 1998.

18 R. Benigni, and V. Cerami, *La Vie est belle*, Paris: Gallimard, Collection 'Folio', 1998, p. 251.

19 Georges Perec, *Cantarix Sopranica L. et autres écrits scientifiques*, Paris: Seuil, Collection 'Points', 2007, p. 61, no. 17; p. 56, n. 12.

20 Georges Perec, *W, or The Memory of Childhood*, trans. David Bellos, Jaffrey, NH: David R. Godine, 1988, pp. 110–11.

21 Dr H. Münch, former doctor at the Auschwitz Hygiene Institute, interviewed in *Der Spiegel*, cited in *Le Patriote Résistant*, 710 (Dec. 1995), p. 5.

22 H. Derogy, *Une Ligne de chance*, Paris: Fayard, 1998, p. 35.

23 Anne Frank, *The Diary of a Young Girl*, ed. Otto H. Frank and Mirjam Pressler, Harmondsworth: Penguin, 2007. The original Dutch edition appeared in 1947.

24 Sigmund Freud, 'Humour', in *The Standard Edition of the Complete Psychological Works of Sigmund Freud*, 24 vols, London: Hogarth Press/Institute of Psychoanalysis, 1953–73, XXI, p. 162.

25 See John Bowlby, 'Developmental Psychiatry Comes of Age', *American Journal of Psychiatry*, 145 (1988), pp. 1–10.

26 The slogan is E. E. Werner's, cited in S. Wolin and R. Wolin, 'Resilience among Youth Brought up in Substance-Abusing Families', *Pediatric Clinic American*, 42 (1995), pp. 415–29.

27 E. E. Werner and R. S. Smith, *Vulnerable but Invincible: A Longitudinal Study of Resilient Children and Youth*, New York: McGraw-Hill, 1982.

28 N. Loutre du Pasquier, *Le Devenir des enfants abandonnés*, Paris: PUF, 1981.

29 A. Dumaret and M. Coppel-Batsche, 'Evolution à l'âge adulte d'enfants placés en famille d'accueil', *Psychiatrie de l'Enfant*, 2 (1996).

30 M. Duyne, *Les Enfants abandonnés: rôle des familles adoptives et des assistantes maternelles*, Monographies françaises de psychologie 56, Paris: Editions du CNRS, 1981.

31 J. Kaufman and E. Zigler, 'Do Abused Children Become Abusive Parents?', *American Journal of Ortho-Psychiatry*, 52 (April 1987), p. 2.

32 R. Bourois, 'Resistance et autodestruction dans l'apartheid américain', *Actes de la Recherche en Sciences Sociales*, 120 (Dec. 1997).

33 R. Robinson, 'The Present State of People who Survived the Holocaust as Children', *Acta Psychiatrica Scandinavia*, 89 (1994), pp. 242–5.

34 See L. Azmentier, *Dictionnaire de la théorie et de l'histoire littéraire du XIXe siècle à nos jours*, Paris: Retz, 1986.

35 S. Freud, 'Notes Upon a Case of Obsessional Neurosis (The "Rat Man")', in *Complete Works*, X, p. 191.

36 André Ughetto, 'La "morale" de l'oxymoron dans *Les Fleurs du mal*', in *Analyse et réflexion: Baudelaire, Spleen et idéal*, Paris: Ellipses, 1984.

37 Charles Baudelaire, 'The Clock', in *The Flowers of Evil*, trans. with notes by James MacGowan, intro. Jonathan Culler, Oxford: Oxford World's Classics, 1993, pp. 161–2.

38 Baudelaire, 'You'd entertain the universe …', ibid., p. 54.

39 Geneviève Anthonioz-de Gaulle, *La Vie en face*, Arte TV, broadcast 1 Dec. 1998.

40 Geneviève Anthonioz-de Gaulle, *La Traversée de la nuit*, Paris: Seuil, 1998.

41 In V. Colin-Simard, 'Entretien avec Geneviève Anthonioz-de Gaulle', *Elle*, 30 Nov. 1998.

42 Jorge Semprun, *Adieu, vive clarté*, Paris: Gallimard, 1998, p. 92.

43 Jean Genet, *The Thief's Journal*, trans. Bernard Frechtman, Harmondsworth: Penguin, 1967, p. 9.

44 Cited in M. Lemay, 'Ces Enfants qui tiennent le coup', in Boris Cyrulnik, ed., *Ces Enfants qui tiennent le coup*, Revigny-sur-Ornain: Hommes et Perspectives, 1998.

45 C. F. Baddoura, 'Traverser la guerre', in Boris Cyrulnik, ed., *Ces Enfants qui tiennent le coup*, Revigny-sur-Ornain: Hommes et Perspectives, 1998.

46 R. Coutance, 'Ligue Française pour la Santé Mentale', *Journées UNESCO*, 1992.

47 Eva Hedlund, 'L'Expérience suédoise du traitement des aggressions sexuelles. Quelles difficultés après vingt ans de travail?', paper presented at conference 'Le Viol, un crime,

vivre après', Collectif Féministe contre la Viol, Ecole Nationale de la Magistrature, 24 Jan. 1995, p. 43.

48 The lawyer Serge Klarsfeld (born Bucharest, 1935) was instrumental in locating the whereabouts of two senior Gestapo officers. His tireless archival work is one of the most precious resources for the study of the Holocaust in France. Klarsfeld's father was deported and killed in an extermination camp. [DM]

49 C. Koupernik, 'Plaidoyeur pour le cas unique', *Pour la Recherche*, 2 (March 1998).

II Hope Where None Might Be Expected

1 N. Auriat, 'Les Défaillances de la mémoire humaine', *Cahier INED*, 136 (1996).

2 The incident occurred on 13 May 1993. [DM]

3 L. Bailly, *Les Catastrophes et leur conséquences psychotraumatiques chez l'enfant*, Paris; ESF, 1996, p. 59.

4 The unfinished housing estate at Drancy, a few miles north of Paris, was used as a transit camp. Between 1942 and 1944, 70,000 people, most of them Jews, were deported from here to Auschwitz. Fewer than 2,000 survived. [DM]

5 The former Communist Jacques Doriot (1898–1945) was the founder of the fascist Parti Populaire Français and an active collaborator with the Germans. He subsequently fought on the Russian front with the German army. [DM]

6 E. M. Cioran in *Magazine Littéraire*, 327 (Dec. 1994), p. 19.

7 Holmes and Rahe's social adjustment scales, in C. André, F. Lelord and P. Légeron, *Le Stress*, Toulouse: Privat, 1998, p. 19.

8 Michel Laurent, *Je pense à vous*, Paris: Seuil, 1995.

9 Charlotte Delbo, *Auschwitz and After*, trans. Rosette C. Lamont, intro. Lawrence L. Langer, New Haven and London: Yale University Press, 1995, pp. 277–8.

10 Sidney Stewart, *Give Us This Day*, New York and London: Norton, 1999; personal communication from Joyce MacDougal.

11 Boris Cyrulnik, 'Les Enfants sans lien', in J. Aïn, *Errances*, Paris: ERES, 1996, pp. 30–46.

12 Jean-Paul Sartre, *Words*, trans. Irene Clephane, Harmondsworth: Penguin, 2000, p. 56.

13 John Bowlby, *Attachment and Loss*, vol. III: *Loss, Sadness and Depression*, London: Pimlico, 1998, p. 343.

14 Georges Perec, *W, or The Memory of Childhood*, trans. David Bellos, Jaffrey, NH: David R. Godine, 1988, p. 26.

15 M. Toussignant, *Les Origines sociales et culturelles des troubles psychiques*, Paris: PUF, 1992, p. 225.

16 Y. S. Ben Porath, *Issues in the Psycho-social Adjustment of Refugees*, Minneapolis: University of Minnesota National Institute of Mental Health's Refugee Assistance Program, 1987.

17 Toussignant, *Les Origines*, p. 228.

18 Sigmund Freud, 'The Psycho-Neurosis of Defence' (1894), in *The Standard Edition of the Complete Psychological Works of Sigmund Freud*, 24 vols, London: Hogarth Press/Institute of Psychoanalysis, 1953–73, II.

19 J. M. Berry, K. Vim, T. Minde and D. Mok, 'Comparative Studies of Acculturative Stress', *International Migration Review*, 21 (1987), pp. 491–511.

20 Toussignant, *Les Origines*, p. 233.

21 Elias Canetti, *Crowds and Power*, trans. Carol Stewart, Harmondsworth: Penguin, 1973, p. 265.

22 Ibid.

23 See Nina Sutton, *Bruno Bettelheim: The Other Side of Madness*, trans. David Sharp, London: Duckworth, 1995.

24 Vasily Grossman, *Life and Fate*, trans. Robert Chandler, London: Harvill Press, 1995.

25 E. Prener, *L'Homme coupable: La Folie et la faute en Occident*, Paris: Odile Jacob, 1996.

26 See Didier Anzieu, *The Skin Ego: A Psychoanalytic Approach to the Self*, trans. Chris Turner, New Haven and London: Yale University Press, 1989.

27 A. Hyanal, 'Les Orphelins savent rebondir', in Boris Cyrulnik, ed., *Ces Enfants qui tiennent le coup*, Revigny-sur-Ornain: Hommes et Perspectives, 1998, p. 49.

28 J. M. Porret, 'Orphelinage et créativité', PhD thesis, University of Geneva, 1977.

29 A. Haynal, *Depression et creativite: Le Sens du desespoir*, Lyon: Césura, 1987.

30 N. Boothby, 'Children of War: Survival as a Collective Act', in M. McCallin, ed., *The Psychological Well-Being of Refugee Children*, Geneva: Bureau International Catholique de l'Enfance, 1996.

31 Ibid.

32 R. L. Punamaki, 'Psychological Reactions of Palestinian and Israeli Children toward Violence', in Marianne Kahnert, David Pitt and Ikka Taipale, eds., *Children in War: Proceedings of a Symposium at Siuntio Baths, Finland, 24–27 March 1983*, Jyväskylä: Oy Gummerus Ab, 1983.

33 M. Grappe, 'Troubles psychiques post-traumatiques chez les enfants victimes de la guerre: séquelles simples et formes cliniques graves', *La Revue Française de Psychiatrie et de Psychologie Médicale*, 10 (Sept. 1997), pp. 38–43.

34 R. Sprengel, in R. Fajrajzen, *The Psychological, Educational*

and Social Adjustment of Refugee and Displaced Children in Europe, Geneva: UNESCO, 1952.

35 Grappe, 'Troubles psychiques'.

36 L. Morisseau, 'Un Aspect psychopathologique de la violence dans la guerre chez l'enfant: le clivage individual et collectif dans les traumatismes dans le psychisme et la culture', in B. Doray and C. Louzon, eds., *Les Traumatismes dans le psychisme et la culture*, Paris: ERES, 1997, pp. 185–9.

37 For the development of her views, see Anna Freud, *Selected Writings*, ed. and intro. Richard Evans and Ruth Freeman, Harmondsworth: Penguin, 1998.

38 Marie-Rose Moro, *Psychothérapie transculturelle des enfants des migrants*, Paris: Dunod, 1998, p. 93.

39 M.-R. Moro, 'D'où viennent ces enfants si étranges? Logiques de l'exposition dans la psychopathologie des enfants de migrants', *Nouvelle Revue d'Ethnopsychiatrie*, 12 (1989).

40 Moro, *Psychopathologie transculturelle*, p. 174.

41 The luxury hotel on the boulevard Raspail was one of the main reception centres for the deportees who returned from the camps. [DM]

42 Jorge Semprun, discussing his *Adieu, vive clarté* on *Bouillon de culture*, France 2 TV, broadcast 6 March 1998.

43 Cited, Paul Veyne, 'The Roman Empire', in Philippe Ariès and Georges Duby, eds., *A History of Private Life*, vol. I: *From Pagan Rome to Byzantium*, ed. Paul Veyne, trans. Arthur Goldhammer, Cambridge, MA, and London: The Belknap Press of Harvard University Press, 1987, p. 9.

44 Ibid.

45 Cited ibid., p. 16.

46 A. Burguière, 'La Famille, quelle histoire', *L'Ecole des Parents*, 4 (April 1987).

47 J. E. Le Goff, *Urgences*, 4 (1995), p. 228.

48 J. L. Flandrin, *Famille, parenté, maison, sexualité dans l'ancienne société*, Paris: Hachette, 1976, p. 220.

49 Y. Kniebihler, *Les Pères aussi ont une histoire*, Paris: Hachette, 1987.

50 A. Bassitche, 'L'Evolution des relations familiales comme indicateur de changement social en Côte-d'Ivoire', *Bulletin de l'Association Française de Psychologie et de Psychopathologie Sociale*, Spring 1991.

51 G. Langlois, 'Les Enfants et les parents d'abord', *Impact Medicine*, 30 (Nov. 1998).

52 G. Vigarello, *Histoire du viol, XVe – XXe siècles*, Paris: Seuil, 1998.

53 C. Julien, *L'Inattendu*, Paris: POL, 1992.

54 P. Strauss, 'Maltraitance: qui, pourquoi, comment?', in *L'Enfance maltraitée*, Paris: Syros, 1996.

55 J. Caffey, 'Multiple Fractures in the Long Bones of Infants Suffering from Chronic Subdural Haemotom', *American Journal of Roentgenology*, 56 (1946), pp. 163–73; F. N. Silverman, 'Unrecognized Trauma in Infants, the Battered Child Syndrome and the Syndrome of Ambroise Tardieu', *Radiology*, 104 (1972), pp. 337–53

56 C. H. Kempe et al., 'The Battered Child Syndrome', *Journal of the American Medical Association*, 181 (1962), pp. 17–24.

57 Lieutenant Colonel Masson, Journées UNICEF, La Garde (Var), 5 Nov. 1998.

58 T. Anatrella, conference 'Les Vendredis de Châteauvallon', 1995.

59 D. Baumann, *La Mémoire des oubliés: Grandir après Auschwitz*, Paris: Albin Michel, 1988.

60 P. Strauss and M. Manciaux, *L'Enfant maltraité*, Paris: Fleurus, 1993, pp. 570–71.

61 Serge Moscovici, *Chronique des années égarées*, Paris: Stock, 1997, p. 8.

62 René Spitz, 'Anaclitic Depression', *Psychoanalytic Study of the Child*, 2 (1946), pp. 313–42.

63 Jean Laplanche and J.-B. Pontalis, 'Anaclitic Depression', in *The Language of Psychoanalysis*, trans. Donald Nicholson-Smith, London: Hogarth Press/Institute of Psychoanalysis, 1973, p. 32.

64 Spitz, cited ibid.

65 M. Radke-Yarrow and T. Sherman, 'Hard Growing: Children who Survive', in J. Rolf et al., eds., *Risk and Protective Factors in the Development of Psychopathology*, Cambridge: Cambridge University Press, 1990, p. 98.

66 Y. Michaud, 'La Violence: Une Question de normes', *Sciences Humaines*, 89 (Dec. 1998), pp. 20–25.

67 G. E. Vaillant and C. O. Vaillant, 'Natural History of Male Psychological Health. A 45-year study of Predictors of Successful Aging', *American Journal of Psychiatry*, 147 (1990), pp. 32–7.

68 A. Brauner and F. Brauner, *Le Dessin de l'enfant dans la guerre*, Paris: Expansion Scientifique Française, 1991.

69 Anna Freud, *The Ego and the Mechanisms of Defence*, trans. Cecil Baines, London: Hogarth Press/Institute of Psychoanalysis, 1948, p. 179.

70 Joseph Sandler cited in S. Ionescu, M. M. Jacquet and C. Lhote, *Les Mécanismes de défense*, Paris: Nathan, 1997, p. 205.

71 C. Mignot and P. Strauss, *Etude du devenir à long terme d'une cohorte d'enfants maltraités dans leur première enfance*, Paris: Ministre de la Justice/AFIREM, 1991.

72 Ibid.

73 Dorothy Burlingham and Anna Freud, *Infants Without Families*, New York: International Universities Press, 1944.

74 See Margaret Mead, *Growth and Culture: A Photographic Record of Balinese Childhood*, New York: G. P. Putman's Sons, 1951.

75 Serge Lebovici, 'A Propos des effets lointains des séparations précoces', *Abstracts Neuropsychiatriques*, 145 (March–April 1996), p. 35.

76 H. G. Birch and J. D. Gussow, *Disadvantaged Children: Health, Nutrition and School Failure*, New York: Grune & Stratton, 1970.

77 L. Freden, *Aspects psychosociaux de la dépression*, Brussels: Pierre Mardaga, 1982, pp. 74–6.

78 G. W. Brown, T. O. Harris and A. Bifulco, 'The Long Term Effects of Early Loss of Parent', in M. Rutter, C. E. Izard and P. B. Read, eds., *Depression in Young People*, New York: Guilford Press, 1986.

79 M. Rutter, 'Psychosocial Resilience and Protective Mechanisms', in Rolf et al., eds., *Risk and Protective Factors in the Development of Psychopathology*, p. 193.

80 J.-L. Guettat, ed., *Exploitation d'une enquête auprès d'une centaine d'adolescents sortis de l'IMPRO depuis dix ans*, Montpellier: L'Essor, 1980.

81 G. Balazs, J.-P. Faguer and F. Dossou, *Jeunes et premiers emplois*, Cahiers du Centre d'Etude de l'Emploi 20, Paris: PUF, 1980.

82 D. Quinton, M. Rutter and C. Little, 'Institutional Reading, Parental Difficulties and Marital Support', *Psychological Medicine*, 14 (1984), pp. 107–24.

83 Rutter, 'Psychosocial Resilience', p. 196.

84 M. Lani, 'A la recherche . . . de la génération perdue', *Journal des Psychologues*, March 1990.

85 M. Buyme, *Les Enfants abandonnés: Rôle des familles adoptives et des assistants maternelles*, Monographies françaises

de psychologie 56, Paris: Editions du CNRS, 1981, p. 119.

86 Y. Lejuene, 'Le Village d'enfants en France, 1946: Nouvelle formule enfance-assistance', PhD thesis, Centre de Formation Sociale, Liège, 1946.

87 Ibid., pp. 45–6, 49.

88 J. Meunier, *Les Gamins de Bogotá*, Paris: Métailié, 1989.

89 J.-L. Quettat, 'Pour une prise en charge réelle et réaliste', *L'Essor* (Montpellier: ACDIF), Dec. 1980.

90 Baumann, *La Mémoire des oubliés*, p. 21.

91 Ibid., pp. 188–93 and personal communications.

92 Ibid. and personal communications.

III Black Suns Without Melancholy

1 'Little Red Riding Hood', in *Perrault's Fairy Tales*, trans. A. E Johnson, Ware: Wordsworth Editions, 2004, p. 66.

2 Jean-Paul Sartre, *Words*, trans. Irene Clephane, Harmondsworth: Penguin, 2000, p. 9.

3 Isak Dinesen cited in Hanna Arendt, *The Human Condition*, Chicago: University of Chicago Press, 1998, p. 175.

4 *Kazan on Kazan*, ed. Jeff Young, London: Faber & Faber, 1997; Françoise Dolto, *Autoportait d'une psychanalyste*, Paris: Seuil, 1989; Pierre Jakez Hélias, *The Horse of Pride*, trans. J. Guicharnaud, New Haven and London: Yale University Press, 1978.

5 C. Chauchat, *L'Autobiographie*, Paris: Gallimard, Collection 'Lire', 1993, p. 20.

6 Jean Malaurie: anthropologist, writer and founder of Plon's 'Terre Humaine' collection. [DM]

7 Emile Zola, *Carnets d'enquêtes: Une Ethnographie inédite en France*, Paris: Plon, 1986.

8 J.-L. Lahaye, *Cent familles*, Paris: Editions Carrère, 1985.

9 Sigmund Freud, 'Fragments of An Analysis of a Case of Hysteria ("Dora")', in *The Standard Edition of the Complete Psychological Works of Sigmund Freud*, 24 vols, London: Hogarth Press/Institute of Psychoanalysis, 1953–73, VII, pp. 16–17.

10 Barbara: popular singer (1930–97), pseudonym of Monique Serf. [DM]

11 Claude Rhodain, *Le Destin bousculé*, Paris: Robert Laffont, Collection 'Vécu', 1986.

12 C. Enjolet, *Princesse d'ailleurs*, Paris: Phébus, 1997.

13 John Bowlby, *Attachment and Loss*, vol. III: *Loss, Sadness and Depression*, London: Pimlico, 1998.

14 F. Abalan and M. Bourgeois, 'Les Conséquences neuropsychiques de la déportation', *Synapse*, 119 (1995), p. 53.

15 Pascal Bruckner, *La Tentation de l'innocence*, Paris: Grasset, 1995.

16 Ibid.

17 Ana Novac, *Les Beaux Jours de mon enfance*, Paris: Balland, 1995.

18 Conference, 'Sommes-nous les enfants d'Auschwitz?', Commission Centrale de l'Enfance, Paris, La Sorbonne, 7 June 1998.

19 Georges Perec, *W, or The Memory of Childhood*, trans. David Bellos, Jaffrey, NH: David R. Godine, 1988, p. 19.

20 See Michel Leiris, *Vie et oeuvre*, Paris: Gallimard, 1996.

21 Perec, *W*, p. 19.

22 D. Lebreton, *Passions du risqué*, Paris: Metailié, 1991.

23 Perec, *W*, p. 3.

24 Georges Perec, *Je me souviens*, Paris: Hachette, 1978.

25 Frei (b. 1937) is the son of Jewish Polish immigrants. His parents were deported to the death camps during the Second World War. [DM]

26 Joël Arès, *Le Fils favori*, Paris: Editions du Rocher, 1998.

27 L. Cahill, B. Prins, M. Weber and J. L. McGaugh, 'Beta-adrenergic Activation and Memory for Emotional Events', *Nature*, 371 (1994), pp. 702–4.

28 L. Richard, *Nazisme et littérature*, Paris: Maspero, 1971, p. 18.

29 A. Ziegler in *Völkischer Beobachter*, 14 Jan. 1937, cited in Richard, *Nazisme et littérature*, p. 126.

30 E. Barnavi, ed., *Histoire universelle des Juifs de la Genèse à la fin du XXᵉ siècle*, Paris: Hachette, 1992.

31 See also n. 10. Barbara, *Il était un piano noir: Mémoires interrompus*, Paris: Fayard, 1998, p. 31.

32 Henri Barbusse, *Under Fire: The Story of a Squad*, trans. W. Fitzwater Wray, London: Dent, 1917.

33 Antoine Prost, 'Monuments to the Dead', in Pierre Nora, ed., *Realms of Memory*, vol. II: *Tradition*, trans. Arthur Goldhammer, New York: Columbia University Press, 1997, p. 317.

34 Alain Finkielkraut, *La Mémoire vaine*, Paris: Gallimard, 1989.

35 C. Browning, *Des Hommes ordinaires*, Paris: Les Belles Lettres, 1994.

36 R. Dulong, *Le Témoin oculaire*, Paris: Ecole des Hautes Etudes en Sciences Sociales, 1998, p. 47.

37 G. Namer, *Mémoire et société*, Paris: Méridien-Klincksiek, 1987, p. 143.

38 G. Vigarello, *Histoire du viol, XVᵉ – XXᵉ siècles*, Paris: Seuil, 1998.

39 Robert Antelme, *The Human Race*, trans. Jeffrey Haight and Annie Mahler, Marlboro, VT: Marloboro Press, 1992 (first published in French 1947); David Rousset, *Les Jours de notre mort*, Paris: Editions du Pavois, 1947.

40 B. Poirot-Delpech, *Papon: Un Crime de bureau*, Paris: Plon, 1998.

41 Maurice Papon, *Le Monde de Léa*, TFi TV, broadcast 27 Nov. 1997.

42 Cited in R. Dulong, *Le Témoin oculaire*, p. 112.

43 M. Lafont, 'L'Extermination douce', PhD thesis, University of Lyon, 1981.

44 Alexis Carrel, *Man, The Unknown*, London: Penguin, 1949, pp. 147, 290–91 (first published in France, 1935).

45 Charlotte Delbo, *Auschwitz and After*, trans. Rosette C. Lamont, intro. Lawrence L. Langer, New Haven and London: Yale University Press, 1995, p. 278.

46 Elizabeth Loftus and Katherine Ketcham, *The Myth of Repressed Memory*, New York: St Martin's Press, 1994, p. 4.

47 Tobie Nathan, *L'Influence qui guérit*, Paris: Odile Jacob, 1994; Daniel Bougnoux, ed., *La Suggestion: Hypnose, influence, transe: Colloque de Cerisy*, Chilly-Mazarin: Delagrange, Collection 'Les Empêcheurs de penser en rond', 1998; Jean Léon Beauvois, *Traité de la servitude libérale*, Paris: Dunod, 1994.

48 Beauvois, *Traité de la servitude libérale*.

49 Barbara, 'Nantes', from the album *Dis, Quand Reviendras-tu?* (1963).

50 Ellen Bass and Laura Davis, *The Courage to Heal: A Guide for Women Survivors of Child Sexual Abuse*, New York: Harper & Row, 1988.

51 A. Baddeley, *La Mémoire humaine: Théorie et pratique*, Grenoble: Presses Universitaires de Grenoble, 1993, p. 443.

52 A.-R. Damasio, *L'Erreur de Descartes: La Raison des emotions*, Paris: Odile Jacob, 1995.

53 Boris Cyrulnik, 'La Transmission de pensée ou le comment de la parole', in S. Santi, I. Guaïtella, C. Cavé and G.

Kopncyznski, eds., *Oralité et gestualité, communication multi-modale, interaction*, Paris: L'Harmattan, 1998.

54 J. Cosnier, *Le Retour de Psyché: Critique des nouveaux fonde-ments des la psychologie*, Paris, Desclée de Brouwer, 1998.

55 M. Soulé and Boris Cyrulnik, *L'Intelligence avant la parole*, Paris: ESF, 1998.

56 B. de Boysson-Bardies, *Comment la parole vient aux enfants*, Paris: Odile Jacob, 1996.

57 Z. Zlatine, 'Praxis de l'aphasie: au moment de répondre', *Ornicar?*, 33 (April–June 1985), pp. 65–8.

58 Ibid.

59 Y. Joanette, D. Lafond and A. R. Lecours, 'L'Aphasie de l'aphasique', in J. Ponzion, D. Lafond, R. Degiovannie and Y. Joanette, eds., *L'Aphasiaque*, Quebec: Edisem/Paris: Maloine, 1992, p. 23.

60 Zlatine, 'Praxis de l'aphasie'.

61 Ibid.

62 R. Char, 'Dans l'atelier des poètes', Paris: Gallimard, Collection 'Quarto', 1996, p. 23.

63 R. C. Schank, *Dynamic Memory: A Theory of Learning in Computers and People*, Cambridge: Cambridge University Press, 1981.

64 Nicolas Abraham and Maria Torok, *The Shell and the Kernel: Renewals of Psychoanalysis*, trans. N. T. Rand, Chicago: University of Chicago Press, 1994.

65 P. Niemetzky, C. François and B. Cyrulnik, 'Le Secrete secrète, ou l'éclairage éthologique du secret', *Synapse*, 120 (Nov. 1995), pp. 27–30.

66 French artist and sculptor (1930–2002); her real name was Catherine Marie-Agnès Fal de Saint-Phalle. [DM]

67 'L' Enfance mutilée de Niki de Saint Phalle', *Elle*, 7 March 1994.

68 S. Tisseron, 'L'Héritage insu', paper presented at 'Le Su et l'insu', 30th conference, CNRS-INA, Inathèque de France, March 1995.

69 The theme of 'psychic heritage' is developed in N. Abraham and M. Torok, *The Shell and the Kernel*, ed., trans. and intro. Nicholas T. Rand, Chicago: University of Chicago Press, 1994; S. Tisseron, *La Honte: Psychanalyse d'un lien social*, Paris: Dunod, 1992; and C. Nachin, *Les Fantômes de l'âme*, Paris: L'Harmattan, 1993.

70 S. Tisseron, 'L'Héritage insu: les secrets de famille', *Communications Générations et Filiation*, 59 (1994), pp. 231, 236.

71 J. Altounian, *Ouvrez-moi seulement les chemins de l'Arménie: Un Génocide aux déserts de l'inconscient*, Paris: Les Belles Lettres, 1990.

72 Pierre Vidal-Naquet, Preface to D. G. Chalian, *Tribunal permanent des peuples: Le Génocide des Arméniens*, Paris: Flammarion, 1984.

73 N. Hefter, *Si tu t'en sors . . . Auschwitz 1944–1945*, Paris: Le Découverte, 1992.

74 Eye-witness account, conference, 'Sommes-nous les enfants d'Auschwitz?', Commission Centrale de l'Enfance, Paris, La Sorbonne, 7 June 1998.

75 R. de Beaurepaire, 'Les Mémoires traumatiques de Rachel Yehuda', *Dépression*, 10 (Jan.–Feb. 1998).

76 Ibid.

77 R Yehuda, 'Low Urinary Cortisol Excretion in Holocaust Survivors with Post-Traumatic Stress Disorder', *American Journal of Psychiatry*, 152 (1995), pp. 982–6.

78 P. Legendre, *L'Inestimable objet de la transmission*, Paris: Fayard, 1985.

79 J. D. Bremmer, 'MRN: Based Measurement of Hippocampal Volume in Patients with Combat-Related Post-Traumatic

Stress Disorder', *American Journal of Psychiatry*, 152 (1995), pp. 973–81.

80 Alexander Solzhenitsyn, *The Gulag Archipelago*, trans. Thomas P. Whitney, London: Collins/Fontana, 1974, p. 143.

81 Interview with Michel de Castillo, *Dimanche en roue libre*, France-Inter radio, broadcast 18 Oct. 1998.

82 H. Le Bras, *Le Démon des origines*, La Tour des Aigues: Editions de l'Aube, 1998.

82 D. Bisson and E. de Schonen, *L'Enfant derrière la porte*, Paris: Grasset, 1993, pp. 53–4, 66.

84 H. Van Gijseghem, 'Réflexions sur la revelation et la rétraction', in Association Française d'Information et de Recherche sur l'Enfance Maltraité (AFIREM), *Secret maintenu, secret dévoilé*, Paris: Karthala, 1994, pp. 307–12.

85 Ibid.

86 L. Salvayre, *La Compagnie des spectres*, Paris: POL, 1997; *Bouillon de culture*, France 2 TV, broadcast 5 Sept. 1997.

87 M. Lemay, 'La Gestion des paradoxes', in AFIREM, *Secret maintenu, secret dévoilé*, pp. 414–15.

88 M. Roussigant, *Les Origines sociales et culturelles des troubles psychologiques*, Paris: PUF, 1992.

89 G. W. Brown and T. Harris, *Depression in Life Events and Illness*, New York: Guilford Press, 1988.

90 J. A. Flaherty, R. Kohn, I. Levav and S. Birz, 'Demoralization in Soviet-Jewish Immigrants to the United States and Israel', *Comprehensive Psychiatry*, 28(6) (1988), pp. 588–97.

91 V. Last and H. Klein, 'Impact de l'Holocaust; transmission aux enfants du vévu des parents', *Evolution Psychiatrique*, 462 (1981), pp. 373–88.

92 N. Zajde, *Souffle sur tous ces morts*, Paris: Odile Jacob, 1997.

93 N. Monbet, ONG Santé, Marseille, 1998; F. Sironi, Association Primo Levi, Paris.

94 S. Freud, 'Preface to Marie Bonaparte's *The Life and Work of Edgar Allan Poe: A Psychoanalytic Interpretation*', in *Complete Works*, XXII, p. 254.

95 André Haynal, *Dépression et créativité: Le Sens du désespoir*, Lyon: Césura, 1987.

96 Ibid.

97 S. Freud, 'Thoughts on War and Death', *Complete Works*, XIV, p. 291.

98 J. Bruner, *Car la culture donne forme a l'esprit: De La Revolution cognitive a la psychologie culturelle*, Paris: Eshel, 1991, p. 63.

99 See Jean-Paul Sartre, *Saint Genet, Actor and Martyr*, trans. Bernard Frechtman, London: W. H. Allen & Co., 1964.

100 Alain Finkielkraut, *In the Name of Humanity: Reflections on the Twentieth Century*, trans. J. Friedlander, London: Pimlico, 2001, p. 78.

101 Alexander Solzhenitysn, 'The Nobel Prize Lecture on Literature', cited ibid.

102 M Soulé, 'Le Secret de Polichinelle', in AFIREM, *Secret maintenu, secret dévoilé*, pp. 109–24.

103 Elie Wiesel, *Tous les fleuves vont à la mer: Mémoires I*, Paris, Seuil. 1994.

104 Perec, *W*, p. 42.

105 M. Weill, 'Les Blues des femmes de lettres', *Abstracts Neuropsychiatriques*, 130 (15–30 April 1995).

106 A. M. Ludwig, 'Mental Illness and Creative Activity in Female Writers', *American Journal of Psychiatry*, 151 (1994), pp. 1650–56.

107 F. R. de Chateaubriand, *Mémoires d'outre-tombe*, and Talleyrand, *Correspondance*, both cited in Y. C. Blanchom, 'Les Etats dépressifs d'enfance', *Abstracts Neuropsychiatriques*, 174 (30 Nov.–15 Dec. 1997).

108 C. Miollan, 'Quand l'enfant abandonnique crée', *Journal des Psychologues*, 95 (1992), p. 50.

109 S. Ionescu, M.-M. Jacquet and C. Lhote, *Les Mécanismes de défense: théorie et clinique*, Paris: Nathan Université, 1997, p. 249.

110 Gaston Bachelard, *The Poetics of Reverie*, trans. Daniel Russel, Boston: Beacon Press, 1971, p. 157.

111 Paul Watzlawick, *Faites vous-mêmes votre malheur*, Paris: Seuil, 1984.

112 C. Burgelin, *Les Parties de dominos chez M. Lefèvre: Perec avec Freud, Perec contre Freud*, Paris: Circé, 1996, p. 64.

113 Perec, *W*, p. 42.

114 Ibid. pp. 4, 42.

IV Conclusion

1 M. Cioran, *Oeuvres*, Paris: Gallimard, Collection 'Quarto', 1995, p. 47.

2 Georges Fischer, *Le Ressort invisible: Vivre à l'extrême*, Paris: Seuil, 1994, p. 269.

3 A. Bloom and S. Vanistendael, *La Résilience ou le réalisme de l'espérance: Blessé, mais pas vaincu*, Les Cahiers du BICE, Geneva: Bureau International Catholique de l'Enfance, 1996, p. 17.

Contemporary ... Provocative ... Outrageous ...
Prophetic ... Groundbreaking ... Funny ... Disturbing ...
Different ... Moving ... Revolutionary ... Inspiring ...
Subversive ... Life-changing ...

What makes a modern classic?

At Penguin Classics our mission has always been to make the best
books ever written available to everyone. And that also means
constantly redefining and refreshing exactly what makes a 'classic'.
That's where Modern Classics come in. Since 1961 they have been an
organic, ever-growing and ever-evolving list of books from the last
hundred (or so) years that we believe will continue to be read over and
over again.

They could be books that have inspired political dissent, such as
Animal Farm. Some, like *Lolita* or *A Clockwork Orange*, may have
caused shock and outrage. Many have led to great films, from *In Cold
Blood* to *One Flew Over the Cuckoo's Nest*. They have broken down
barriers – whether social, sexual, or, in the case of *Ulysses*, the
boundaries of language itself. And they might – like *Goldfinger* or
Scoop – just be pure classic escapism. Whatever the reason, Penguin
Modern Classics continue to inspire, entertain and enlighten millions
of readers everywhere.

'No publisher has had more influence on reading habits than Penguin'
Independent

'Penguins provided a crash course in world literature'
Guardian

The best books ever written

PENGUIN (🐧) CLASSICS

SINCE 1946

Find out more at www.penguinclassics.com